MAXIMS OF

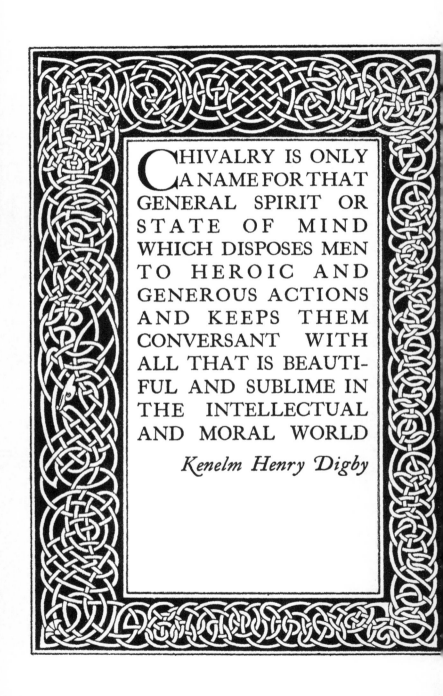

CHIVALRY IS ONLY
A NAME FOR THAT
GENERAL SPIRIT OR
STATE OF MIND
WHICH DISPOSES MEN
TO HEROIC AND
GENEROUS ACTIONS
AND KEEPS THEM
CONVERSANT WITH
ALL THAT IS BEAUTI-
FUL AND SUBLIME IN
THE INTELLECTUAL
AND MORAL WORLD

*Kenelm Henry Digby*

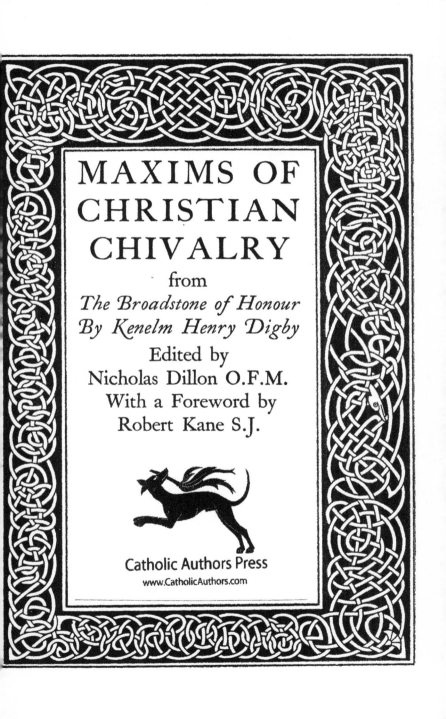

# MAXIMS OF CHRISTIAN CHIVALRY

from
*The Broadstone of Honour*
*By Kenelm Henry Digby*
Edited by
Nicholas Dillon O.F.M.
With a Foreword by
Robert Kane S.J.

Catholic Authors Press
www.CatholicAuthors.com

IMPRIMI POTEST : Fr. Rogerius Moloney, O.F.M.,
NIHIL OBSTAT : Gulielmus Harpur, *Censor Dep:*
IMPRIMATUR : ✠ Gulielmus, *Episcopus Fernensis.*

Wexfordiæ, die 12 Octobris, 1925.

*First Edition...*      *1924*
*Reprinted......*      *2003*

Catholic Authors Press
P.O. Box 370365
W. Hartford, CT 06137

# DEDICATION

TO THE GLORIOUS
VIRGIN MARTYR OF CHRIST
ST. PHILOMENA
THESE PAGES ARE
EVERENTLY AND GRATEFULL
DEDICATED

# CONTENTS

# FOREWORD

HERE IS AN IDEAL FOR WHICH true men live, and for which, if need were, they would die. Not to its profit do they look or to any material gain that it can give. Its power over them comes not from pleasure, nor is ambition the secret mainspring of its strength. Without it, wealth has no worth, pleasure no charm, fame no fascination, success no crown. Without it, prosperity crumbles to the value of the dust, and all the finer flowers of human life wither beneath the breath of bitter but just contempt. With it, misfortune may become noble, suffering worshipful, disaster magnificent. It can give to trifles a preciousness greater than gold can buy ; it can transform hardship into happiness ; and round the worst failure it can throw the glory of a true triumph. For, ideal though it be, it has a strange practical power. It is the one test which inexorably unmasks the liar, the knave, or the animal, amongst men, and which faithfully reveals the true, the good, and the noble. It is Honour.

Honour is not the mere absence of what is false, unfair, or foul ; nor is it only the presence of perfect accuracy in truth, of perfect balance in justice, and of perfect becomingness in conduct.

Thus Honour has a triple aspect, as it regards truth, right, and conduct. But again, under each of these aspects it means much more than what is true, good, worthy. It means what, under each of these aspects, is excellent, refined, noble. It means the *highest* reverence for truth, the *deepest* devotedness to right, and the *brightest* chivalry in conduct.

It is more than a dutiful obedience to truth and right. Honour is a chivalrous allegiance, an enthusiastic loyalty, a death-daring devotedness, to what in truth is most delicate and to what in right is most refined. A man of honour is a hero of the highest type and of the most sterling worth.

There is a secondary and consequent meaning attached to the word "honour" as it is taken to express the recognition, esteem, and admiration, deserved by and given to a man of honour. But this knowledge and praise is a homage rendered to Honour. It is not Honour itself. A man of honour is not a hero because he is praised, but he is rightly praised because he is truly a man of honour.

In those Middle Ages, which are called dark, when the learning and literature of the past were almost submerged under a deluge of barbaric storm, and would have irretrievably perished had their records not been hidden and safely stored in the monasteries of peaceful and prayerful monks, there was yet a light which grew brighter as the gloom around grew blacker, a light that had been kindled within men's souls by a fire that came from heaven, the light of Honour, that was fanned by divine faith till it reached the glorious radiance of Christian Chivalry.

A great man, who, with the patient and persistent labour of a monk, with the keenness and research of a scientist, with the taste and appreciation of an artist, with the wide synthesis and accurate balance of a master-mind, had also the serene nobility and enthusiastic devotedness of a true Knight-Errant, Kenelm Digby, understood all this. He also understood how feeble and faint that light of Honour is in this poor paltry age of ours, when wealth, pleasure, art that is sensuous, and science that is material, liberty that is let loose to licence, and authority that is made the slave of whim, are looked upon as worshipful, while Honour is most often looked upon as at most a mere ornament, an honour that is the empty praise of men's mouths, the applause of the rabble, or the fashion of fools, a title that may be bought or sold for money or for ignoble service. Yet he further understood that even now there is in true Honour a charm that can captivate the mind which is open, frank, and eager for light, and that can appeal to the soul which is pure, brave, and enamoured of what is noble. He therefore wrote The Broadstone of Honour.

But that book, big, wide, deep, as it is, is too heavy and hard for many who would yet like to know the talisman enclosed in it. Father Nicholas Dillon, my dear old pupil of Clongowes Wood, has endeavoured to bring some of its treasures within our reach in this book of his, the " Maxims of Christian Chivalry." To my mind he has succeeded.

Nay ! Nay ! Chivalry is not dead, even in our days of sordid thought and selfish aim. It only slumbers. It will awaken, careless of all gain, defiant of all danger, devoted, impetuous, enthusiastic as ever crusader, when a man recognizes his vocation to personal honour, and much more when a people is inspired and becomes heroic at the call of national honour.

In the hope of helping the reader to pick out at once some typical passages which would give him a general idea of the book, and might entice him to study more, I suggest some references to the Maxims of Christian Chivalry :

Definition of Honour, pages 32.
Definition of Chivalry, p. 3.
Motto of Chivalry, p. 98.
The dignity which Chivalry required, p. 100.
The feelings of Chivalry, p. 129.
Rules of Chivalry, pp. 47 and 48.
Extracts from Book of Chivalrous Instruction, p. 43.
Passages referring to Knighthood, p. 18.
Religious Orders of Knighthood, p. 127.
Preparation for Knighthood, p. 72.
List of famous Knights, p. 35.

ROBERT KANE S.J.

# *INTRODUCTION*

T MAY BE SAID THAT THIS LITTLE book has not the literary form or plan or arrangement which books ought to have. But what it lacks in point of form is more than made up for by worth of a higher kind. For God's Truth is one, it is free as the sunshine, as the bounding waves of the ocean. The Broadstone of Honour is no literary garden, no well planned out plantation. It is a forest primeval, or medieval. The sunshine which streams through its branches is God's own Truth, its pine-music is waked by a wind which comes from a shoreless sea. It has vistas and wood-voices enough if you have soul-eyes to see and soul-ears to hear. But in this forest is no place for sign-post or hedgerow, or roadway, far less for our mad world's loud chorus of falsehood and vulgarity. Leave these things behind you. Enter at once into the trackless forest depths of The Broadstone of Honour. Come and listen. Come and see.

The object of this little book is threefold : to rescue from almost total oblivion the memory of a glorious man whose name is almost forgotten ; to give some notion of the grandeur of his first great work The Broadstone of Honour ; and, so far as may be done in these few pages, to make it possible to have some glimpse of the inmost soul of those grand Middle Ages, which are said to cover a thousand years from the fifth to the fifteenth century.

Kenelm Henry Digby was born in Ireland at Geashill in King's County, almost exactly at the beginning of the nineteenth century. His father, William Digby, was

## Introduction

Protestant rector of that place. Educated at the University of
Cambridge, Kenelm had scarcely passed the years of boyhood
when, with tremendous zeal and ardour, he plunged into the
study of the history and literature of the Middle Ages. Before
he became a Catholic he wrote and published, in short form,
his first great work The Broadstone of Honour, a book which
contains the fruit of an amount of reading and thought
which might well be enough for the life's labour of an ordinary
man of letters. After his conversion to the Catholic Faith
he re-wrote, in an enlarged form and in an intensely Catholic
sense and spirit, this wonderful book. It was probably
in one of the last months of 1825 that Fr. Scott, S.J. received
Kenelm Digby into the Church. During the rest of his long
and laborious life his lot was cast for the most part in England
and France, in which countries mainly he collected the immense treasures of history and literature which sufficed for
the numerous volumes which he published. In 1833 he
married an Irish Catholic lady, of whom it is enough here
to say that she was worthy of her husband. Kenelm Henry
Digby died on March 22nd, 1880. He is certainly entitled
to rank with De Maistre and Don Garcia Moreno as one of
the first Catholic laymen of the nineteenth century.

Bernard Holland, C.B. brought out in 1919 a beautiful
memoir of Kenelm Henry Digby.

In the year 1825 a son of St. Ignatius received Kenelm
Digby into the Church, Mother, Mistress, and Guardian, of
Christian Chivalry. Surely then, for more reasons than
one, it is fitting that in 1925 the much loved name of Fr.
Robert Kane, S.J. should be written on this little wreath
before it lies on Digby's grave.

THE EDITOR.

# The Book of Godefridus

# The Book of Godefridus

Y FIRST ENDEAVOUR WILL BE to give a general idea of the views and principles respecting Chivalry which have guided me in the composition of this work. And as there will be here some express mention of degrees of rank and of Christian government, this book will be presented under the name of that illustrious hero, Godfrey of Bouillon. For his kingly rule seems to have corresponded with the very ideal of perfection in the social order, and his personal qualities were so heroic that, according to an ancient chronicle, an infidel king was heard to say that : " If all the honour of the world were come to an end and lost, Duke Godfrey would have enough of honour in himself to be able to bring it back and raise it aloft." The ground being thus prepared the foundation will be laid in the second book, which will contain a view of the religion and the discipline which belonged to Chivalry in the heroic age of Christianity ; and the name of Tancred suggests itself as that of a representative of that spirit. This will unavoidably lead to a consideration of the objections which have been urged by various sects of innovators against the principles and practice of the Christian Chivalry. And so in the third book, which will be called Morus, after the great chancellor of England Thomas More (now Blessed) who laid down his life to defend the glorious standard of Christ, some of these objections will be examined. In the fourth book the main subject will be resumed by giving a more detailed view of the virtues of the chivalrous character when it was submitted to the genuine and all-powerful influence of the Catholic

faith ; and Orlandus is a name which may be symbolical of this more generous Chivalry.

### The noblest inheritance :

As Friedrich Schlegel says : " Such national recollections, the noblest inheritance which a people can possess, bestow an advantage which no other riches can supply. For when a people are exalted in their feelings and ennobled in their own estimation by the consciousness that they have been illustrious in ages that are gone by, that these recollections have come down to them from a remote and heroic ancestry, in a word, that they have a national poetry of their own, we are willing to acknowledge that their pride is reasonable, and they are raised in our view by the same circumstance which gives them elevation in their own."

### Inspiration from history :

Certainly the more men reflect upon the noble and joyous images presented in heroic history the more they will feel themselves confirmed in all those holy feelings which only can give them dignity and security. The more they think of these things the more they will become persuaded that the principles which those examples illustrate and recommend are the most important that can be made the subject of their study. And so they will see that they can be happy and honourable, can obtain the blessing of God Almighty for themselves, for their country, and for mankind, only in proportion as they adhere to those principles.

### The practice of virtue :

It was no doubt with a high object that most of the writings connected with Chivalry were composed. The practice of virtue was the end proposed by Sir Thomas Malory, who concludes his preface : " Humbly beseeching all noble lords and ladies, with all other estates, of what estate or degree they be of, that shall see and read in this book, that they take the good and honest acts in their remembrance, and to follow the same. Wherein they shall find many joyous and pleasant histories, and noble and renowned acts of humanity, gentleness, and chivalry. For herein may be seen noble chivalry, courtesy, humanity, friendliness, hardiness, love, friendship, cowardice, murder, hate, virtue, and sin. Do after the good, and leave the evil, and it shall bring you to good fame and renown. All is written for our doctrine, and for to beware that we fall not to vice or sin, but to exercise and follow virtue, by which we may come and attain to good fame and renown in this life, and after this short and transitory life to come unto everlasting bliss in heaven, the which He grant us that reigneth in heaven, the Blessed Trinity. Amen."

### The sense of right and wrong :

There have been always passions and errors and consequently crimes and troubles. But it seems to me that the distinction is singularly happy which has been made between the past and later ages on the ground that in the past men knew what was evil and what was good whereas at present many men find it rather hard to be clear as to what is evil and what is good.

### A fault in modern schools :

Laurentie complains of the direction of early studies, which in modern times have been so much devoted to the literary associations of Greece and Rome. A most just complaint, which speaks the sentiment of common sense and piety. In the monastic schools of the Middle Ages, as in those of Chivalry, youths were not brought up as if they were to be Greek and Roman patriots and pagan moralists. While they were induced to respect the virtues of the heathens they felt assured of possessing a far higher standard of conduct and of being bound to the discharge of very different duties. Thus their sentiments, their deeds, their very language, were to be chivalrous, but also essentially Christian. Otherwise, they would have been wanting in regard to Chivalry, which must ever be directed by the highest known good. They were not so blinded by immoderate admiration for classical learning as to look with reverence to the Areopagus or the Forum and to extol the deeds of atrocious wickedness and democratic tyranny which were associated with them.

### What is Chivalry ?

Chivalry is only a name for that general spirit or state of

mind which disposes men to heroic and generous actions and keeps them conversant with all that is beautiful and sublime in the intellectual and moral world. It will be found that this spirit more generally prevails in youth than in the later periods of mens' lives. As the heroic age is commonly the earliest age in the history of nations, so youth, the first period of human life, may be considered as the heroic or chivalrous age of each separate man. And there are few so unhappy as to have grown up without having experienced this influence and having derived the advantage of being able to enrich their imaginations and to soothe their hours of sorrow with its romantic recollections. The Anglo-Saxons distinguished the period between childhood and manhood by the term " cnihthad," boyhood ; a term which still continued to indicate the connection between youth and Chivalry when knights were styled children, as in the historic song beginning :

Child Rowland to the dark tower came.

This is an excellent expression, no doubt ; for every boy and youth ought to be in his mind and sentiments a knight, and essentially a son of Chivalry. Nature is fine in him.

Nothing but the circumstance of a most singular and unhappy constitution or the most perverted and degrading system of education can ever totally destroy the action of this general law. Therefore, as long as there shall be a succession of sweet springs in man's intellectual world, as long as there shall be young men to grow up to maturity, and as long as all youthful life shall not be dead and its source withered for ever, so long must there continue to be the spirit of noble Chivalry.

### Shun the base and ignoble :
From the love of excellence is inseparable a spirit of uncompromising detestation for everything base and criminal. Thus Froissart describes Gaston de Foix, who " in every thyng was so parfite, that he cannot be praised too moche ; he loved that ought to be beloved, and hated that ought to be hated." And he adds a testimony as to his practice, that " he never had myscreant with hym."

4

**Personal responsibility :**

We ought here to observe the operation of a principle which acted as great a part in the moral world of Chivalry as in its political world.   This principle is the consciousness of personal obligations, and therefore, in some sense, of personal importance.   It is the conviction that there is a spiritual monarchy constituting for each man individually the kingdom of his soul in which he has to govern according to truth and justice and to oppose error and evil without regard to the policy of other powers.   Friedrich Schlegel has made some excellent observations on the danger of abandoning this principle in relation to all the great duties of life.   His words are these : " The point wherein human charity chiefly fails is in its being too much concerned with general views and grand abstractions but not sufficiently exercised in the little details of daily life, in the innumerable cases of trouble and care in relieving which it might be employed.   As with the charity so it is with the faith of men ; it is not sufficiently personal, it is not sufficiently confiding.   The greater number of men have by far too high an opinion of their own worth and too great a confidence in their own strength, but of their own vocation, of the end to which they are destined, they have, in general, a sense far too low.   They do not believe in it ; they look upon their calling and destiny and themselves as from the point whence they survey the whole world.   But in this they are guilty of a great error and of a great injustice ; for every man is a separate world in himself, a true micro-cosmus in the eyes of God and in the plan of the whole creation. Every man has a separate calling and an end peculiar to himself."   As in the warfare of the Middle Ages, when each man was regarded as a power, so in the spiritual combats of all times, Chivalry requires every man to believe that he is personally called upon to pronounce between error and truth, injustice and justice, vice and virtue.

**Chivalry immortal :**

What is accidental and not necessarily connected with the inmost soul of Chivalry may indeed have its destined period, beyond which it may be obsolete and lifeless.   The plumed troop and the bright banner and all quality, pride, pomp, and circumstance, of feudal manners may pass with the age which required them, but what essentially belongs to this great cause must endure to the end. Although all other things are uncertain, perishable, and liable to change, this is grafted upon deep and indestructible roots which no time can weaken and no force remove.

### King of the free, generous, and heroic :

" Every one that is of the truth, heareth my voice" (1), said Christ to Pilate ; and we may set this down as a certain consequence, that, excepting in cases of unavoidable ignorance where this Orient from on high hath not dawned in hostility to the world's claims, OUR SAVIOUR JESUS CHRIST HAS BECOME THE CHIEF AND ETERNAL KING OF ALL THE REALLY FREE, GENEROUS, AND HEROIC SPIRITS THAT EXIST UPON THE EARTH (2). So that to Him alone they come, offering homage of undivided love, and renouncing allegiance to the world, scorning its pretensions, and regarding with the utmost degree of contempt and detestation its haughty standard of false honour and false liberty and false virtue. To His Church they repair, from every region and language and people, to confirm their union, to proclaim their fidelity, to take up the arms with which they are to fight against the ruler of this world, to secure their deliverance from the hands of their enemies, and to receive power from their adorable Lord, Who is enthroned in the centre of their hearts, to serve him without fear all their days, in holiness and justice.

### Useless talk :

" Those who speak the most of God," says an old writer in his life of St. Elzear of Sabran, " are very often those who love Him the least. All their virtue vanishes in an excess of useless talk and goes off in a smoke of words."

### Daily Mass :

As long as men were in the most noble quest of Chivalry they were charged " to hear Mass daily, if they may do it ; and that they take upon them to forsake sin." Men were even reminded that all the faithful, after being washed in the healing waters of baptism are called priests, but especially the just, who have the Spirit of God and are made living members of Jesus Christ. For these, by faith, which is kindled by charity, immolate on the altar of their mind spiritual hosts to God (3).

They had read in " The Festival," which was the devotional book of the English laity before the change of religion, " that of those who go to Mass every step thitherward and homeward an angel shall reckon."

### The right internationalism :

It was a disposition absolutely required by Chivalry to seek a union and fellowship with the generous and heroic men of every country.

### Holy priesthood :

In these days when monasteries are described as the monuments of superstition and governments are obliged to build prisons which enclose as much space as a village would occupy, giving rise to a new order of architecture, we hear a great deal of the evils resulting from subjection to the priesthood. The baseness of such a subjection, the shamefulness of recognizing priestly authority, form the favourite theme of the proud sensualists who employ their thoughts upon inventing new sources of pleasure and profit for themselves and new modes of punishment for the poor. The fact, however, is, that I may express it without being tedious, and, as Socrates would say, that I may speak after the manner of geometricians, in proportion as men revere persons of this blessed order we may conclude that they have advanced in virtue. The degree of reverence which is shown for the priesthood is the most faithful criterion by which we may determine how far any age or nation has attained to goodness and sanctity. With what profound humility does it become ordinary men to make mention of so high and mysterious an institution. Our Lord Himself was the first priest in the time of grace, typically foreshadowed by Melchisedech. Oh how reverently do the ancient Fathers speak of priesthood ! Nazianzen says a priest is a mediator between God and man (4). St. John Chrysostom says : " Neither man nor Angel nor Archangel nor any created power but the Paraclete Himself has established this office (5). St. Ambrose says : " Man imposes the hands : but God bestows the grace."(6). And Pacianus says : " How can any society or company of men receive the Holy Ghost if the anointed priest does not sign and bless them ? "

### Love against selfishness :

" Europe," says Schlegel, " was united in one during these grand ages, and the soil of this general country was fruitful in generous thoughts which served to guide both in life and in death. One common Chivalry converted adversaries into brethern in arms, and it was to defend one common faith that that they were armed. Love inspired every heart, and the poetry which sang this alliance expressed the same sentiment in different languages. Alas ! the noble energy of the ancient time is lost. Our age is the inventor of a narrow policy, and what weak men are unable to conceive is in their eyes only a chimera. Nothing that is divine can succeed when it is undertaken with a profane heart. Alas ! our age has knowledge of neither faith nor love. How then could it have preserved hope ?"

### Men shall be lovers of themselves :

1. " Know also this," says the Apostle, " that in the last days, shall come on dangerous times. 2. Men shall be lovers of themselves."(7). That these times had come in our heroic age it was impossible to suppose. But a new period of the world's history has commenced and new principles are said to be necessary. The ancient Orders of Christendom are superseded by clubs and associations whereby men can enjoy some of the pleasures of society without fulfilling the duties attached to social life and in which they may escape the burthen of personal obligation without forfeiting their rights and honour. That love which was the soul of Chivalry, that devoted affection of the youthful heart in conformity with nature's law, which expelled every selfish thought and wish and refined and developed every generous virtue, is exposed to the counteracting influence of the new philosophy. That philosophy teaches the young that there may be happiness without the exercise of virtue, without men being devoted and faithful, disinterested and sincere. It places avarice and ambition (for the passion for wealth is avarice and the love of

rank and high connection is ambition) in the inmost sanctuary of the human heart, and thus defiles in its noblest feature the image of the Almighty. It leads its disciples to regard all duty and obligation, "which gray-beards call divine," as matters in which they have no concern and to say to their selfish hearts like Shakespeare's Richard :

I am myself alone.

The convenience and profit of individuals, not the everlasting distinctions of right and wrong, are consulted and regarded as the only public good ; riches and presumption overpower the opposite scale of virtue and modesty. In a word, the principles and thoughts of men have changed with their political standing. What was once honourable is now said to be obsolete and worthless, imaginary, eccentric and ridiculous ; what was once baseness and crime is now prudence and moderation and philosophy. The question will therefore again present itself to every lover of his species, to every thoughtful observer who casts a philosophic eye upon the character and transactions and interests of mankind, and to him it will indeed be a subject of serious inquiry, how far this new direction which has been given to the movement of the human heart, how far the principles and temper which now influence the actions of men may fulfil the prediction of Holy Scripture : " Men shall be lovers of themselves."

**Three holy powers :**

In his " Philosophy of Life " Schlegel says : " There are three powers in human life and in human society which have a symbolical meaning and a character of sanctity and which rest upon a divine foundation, the paternal authority, the spiritual or priestly authority, and the kingly authority or highest civil power. The loving care of the earthly father has an analogy to and is a kind of representation of that of the Eternal Father, and the respect and obedience due to the former, founded upon nature and sanctioned by revelation, are found more or less in all ages and nations. The spiritual or priestly power, as dispensing the divine grace of Him Who came to save the world, is in the highest degree holy. The judicial or regal power derives a sanctity from its functions of justice and from its Author. Each one of these three holy powers has a kind of analogy and inward relationship towards the others. The father speaks of rule, the ruler of paternal care, while both these are encompassed, as it were, by the spiritual power, holy and venerable, to guide and moderate them. In a word, upon nature, upon divine revelation, and upon historical justice, these three holy powers are grounded, that of the good and loving father, of the pious priest, and of the just king " (or ruler).

### Religion and art :

In the same " Philosophy of Life " we find the following beautiful and profound remark : " If it were conceivable that at any time religion should entirely cease to exist, that not merely its positive plan and revelation should be forgotten but also that in general all faith in the divine, all this sense of a higher unearthly struggle, could be effaced, that this tone of eternity should be silenced in the sensitive breast of the human race, then immediately would all higher art itself perish and disappear. In our age the case is rather the reverse of this. During the general prevailing political unbelief, which is a natural consequence of religious unbelief, the whole of man's life, especially the external part, is no longer understood and regarded according to its symbolical meaning. Therefore, the civil state with all the greatness which once belonged to it has lost much of its ancient venerable splendour and of its former sanctity, while the religious sentiment itself, in reality still existing, is more or less dissipated in party contentions ; so that scarcely can one find any longer a pure, free, condition of simple, pious, faith. It follows that by a great number of men of the cultivated class the arts and the beautiful are regarded as the last remaining emblems of the divine, and as the only palladium of the higher and inward life, though they never can be so in any manner when thus isolated. Our age may be compared in this respect to a formerly rich but now decayed noble house where the only remnants of ancient grandeur are some pieces of family plate and some honourable heir-looms preserved from better times. In like manner our spent and decayed age has preserved only the outward ornaments of art, whilst the great capital of old faith, to which we owe those ornaments and their beauty, as well as its many other good fruits, has been long since consumed for the greatest part of men."

### Heaven on earth :
" Standing upon earth," says St. Augustine, " thou art in heaven when thou lovest God." (8).

### What Chivalry opposes :
In the first place it seems sufficiently clear that Chivalry is essentially opposed to all dispositions of mind and to all schemes of philosophy which are connected in any degree with the passion for ridicule and that ardour for levelling every intellectual and moral degree, which have so generally pre-vailed in all ages and nations when the influence of religion has been observed to decline. I do not allude to that kind of eloquence which Cicero ascribed to Caesar, who could treat of severe subjects with cheerfulness, so that neither a joke was excluded by the greatness of the subject nor yet gravity diminished by the wit. Nor again do I allude to that spirit of ironical pleasantry which distinguished all the writings of the Socratic philosophers, of which we should probably form a wrong idea from viewing their facetious sayings detached from other parts of their works, as they appeared in the collection made by Cato. For such a style and disposition may be very compatible with the noble gravity of which I speak ; though the connection between them may be as diffi-cult to trace as that which is known to exist between indig-nation and laughter. But what is essentially opposed to the spirit of Chivalry is an illiberal, petulant, and indecent, kind of ridicule which is not in accordance with humanity or honour. Or perhaps it would be more just to say, it is a disposition which if examined may disclose the secret of the whole modern character, a character which disposes those who possess it to allow every thought that rises in their mind to grow up and extend to all its consequences, without their being aware of the necessity which may exist for combating it, and crush-ing it as it were in the shell. On a future occasion it will be necessary to show in full detail that, in opposition to such a disposition as this, the heroic character must be involved in

a certain air of majesty and self-possession denoting both joy and sadness, or rather, a sadness which is full of resignation and dignity and peace.

### Baseness helped by ridicule :

" Man has a great dominion over man," says a fine modern writer, " and of all the evils which he can inflict upon his fellow-creatures the greatest, perhaps, is to place the phantom of ridicule between generous feelings and the actions which they would inspire. Love, genius, talent, even grief, all these are exposed to 'the power of irony, and it is impossible to calculate how far the dominion of this spirit may be extended. The admiration of great objects may be laughed away in jest, and he who thinks nothing of importance has the appearance of being above everything. If enthusiasm then does not defend the heart and mind they will permit themselves to be taken hold of on all sides by this aversion to virtue, which unites indolence with gaiety."

### Ruin caused by mockery :

Whatever is most awful and sublime, most eminently generous and beautiful, is exposed chiefly to the base influence of the spirit of ridicule. Were it to prevail there would be nothing left in the world to please the imagination, to exalt the character, or to attract the heart ; there would be nothing in the world really worth living for, and, as a great master of logic has well observed, there would be " never a virtue left to laugh out of countenance." It should never be forgotten that it was with this spirit that Julian the Apostate attacked religion, using not open force as Diocletian had done, which was indeed by this time out of the question, but ridicule and all manner of traitorous arts and reproaches. And thus also in later times the most insidious attempt of the adversaries of the Catholic Church has been to render her contemptible by representing her as responsible for a system incompatible with all higher intellectual accomplishment. But, without any reference to this particular application of the power of ridicule, it is important to remark the evil of the principle itself and its tendency to degrade the youthful mind from the chivalrous dignity of its nature. How is a youth who has been brought up in holy discipline, full of admiration for and confidence in virtue, full of reverence and generosity, to withstand the spirit of ridicule which is incessantly directed by modern writers against all wisdom and goodness ?

**Don Quixote :**

These reflections naturally bring to our recollection the immortal book of Cervantes, which seems at first to rise up in terrible array against all who dare to maintain that the virtues of the chivalrous character are capable of being reduced to practice. No man will be so bold or so insensible as to deny the genius which belonged to the author of *Don Quixote*.

**Ridicule of sentiment :**

Without doubt there is an important lesson to be derived from the whole of *Don Quixote*, the lesson which teaches the necessity of prudence and good sense and moderation, of guarding the imagination from excess of exercise and the feelings from an over-excitement. But this is a lesson to be gently hinted to men of virtue, not to be proclaimed to the profane amidst the mockery of the world. This is not the lesson which the ordinary class of mankind will derive from the book in question ; and, if it were, this is not the lesson of which men stand in need. Sismondi has indeed pronounced in favour of the moral tendency of the whole book, but, while I do not reject his authority, yet having regard to the general character of his principles and to his acknowledging that the moral of the book is profoundly sad, I can never admit the justice of his conclusion. Certainly it will require no prejudice in favour of Chivalry to discern, what may be read by him who runs, that the faults of no age of the world are on the side which incurs the reproach and ridicule of Cervantes. There is no danger in an enlightened age, as it is termed, or truly in any age, of men becoming too heroic, too generous, too zealous in the defence of innocence, too violent in hatred of baseness and crime, too disinterested and too active in the cause of virtue and truth. The danger is quite on the other side. There is much to be feared from the ridicule which is cast upon sentiment, from the importance which is attached to personal convenience, from substituting laws for virtue, and prudence for self-devotion.

### Ridicule ruins Chivalry :

Segur laments that the fine institution of Chivalry should have lost its empire, and that the romance of *Don Quixote*, by its success, and its philosophy concealed under an attractive fiction, should have completed the ruin by fixing ridicule upon even its memory. Cervantes seems to have forseen the effects which his work would produce, when he gives his own opinion in the words of Carasco: " Youngsters read it, grown men understand it, and old people applaud it." Youth saw nothing in it but the beauties derived from the chivalrous and poetical imagination of its author. Grown men discerned his object and rejoiced in being able to play with their own conscience while they made a jest of the inspirations which are for repressing the corrupt passions of the heart.

### Scoffers rebuked :

Cervantes must produce new examples for imitation before he can expect that men will be laughed out of their reverence for those which were the admiration of their fathers ; and indeed the modern despisers of Chivalry must bring forward models of a higher virtue than any which their annals have as yet furnished before the ancient code of humanity will be abandoned by men of honour. Meanwhile the ridicule of the scoffers, when it is not impiously directed against Heaven, is utterly useless with regard to any purpose of moral good ; for it is certain that in these ages men have more need of new fires to be kindled within them and round about them than of anything to restrain their ardour.

### Honour before cold reason :

Friedrich Schlegel shows that it is the feeling, the imagina-tion, the sentiment of honour, rather than reason, which can distinguish the minute line which often separates right from wrong ; and that it is in the cold, abstract, and dead reason, in a dialectic, contentious spirit of argumentation that the first source lies of all errors of belief, and of all corrupt, de-structive thought.

**Source of ridicule :**

It cannot appear strange that Chivalry should be despised and ridiculed if we reflect upon the number of men in these days whose principles are taken from that perplexing and monstrous system of moral philosophy or refined selfishness which has been held and recommended by a numerous class of writers in successive ages of the world, from the Epicureans of old, as represented by Torquatus in Cicero's first book, *De Finibus,* to Hobbes and Paley.

**A right intention :**

It is true, as Aristotle admits, that " Good men, by their very goodness, confer the greatest benefit on themselves "; but, as even this heathen sage observes, " it is not with the view of benefiting themselves that they are good."

**Love God in all things :**

All that is lovely and admirable in this beautiful world, the sweetness of flowers, the clearness of the sky, the cool blue of the placid waters, the solemn recesses of the grove, should be loved in reference to their Author.

**Nature a book :**

According to this philosophy the sources of our knowledge of God cannot be confined to divine revelation and the history of the world. " Nature," says Father Luis of Granada, " is also a book, written on the outside and within, in which the finger of God is visible."

**The grave of youth :**

It is not a poetical fancy but an actual fact which may be verified by daily observation that the philosophy which now so generally prevails has a tendency to blast all intellectual and moral youth and to make young men old, old in selfishness, in avarice old, in love of censure old, in suspicion old, in the general want of belief in any virtue old. It makes them, in the loss of all imagination, of all sense of beauty, and of all reverence, and in the contempt of everything but money and power, like old men who have not escaped the degrading influence of a decayed and world-worn nature.

## Maxims of Christian Chivalry

**Who are the noble ?**

Another philosopher was asked who were noble. He answered ; " Those who despise riches and glory and pleasure and life " ; which is true as and when these things ought to be despised.

**Kings cannot ennoble :**

" The king," says Landor, " may scatter titles and dignities till lords, like the swarm of Dons in Sancho's island, shall become as troublesome as so many flesh-flies, but he cannot save those among whom he scatters them from rottenness and oblivion." The king can give letters of nobility, but he cannot bestow the sentiment which gives virtue to him whom he ennobles. His favour cannot grant the inheritance which is the only one that gives true nobility to an illustrious birth, and his wrath cannot take it away. " The Emperor," says St. Gregory the great, " can make an ape be called a lion, but he cannot make him become one." (9).

**Emperors give riches not nobility :**

The Emperor Sigismund gave this answer to a favourite who begged that he would ennoble him : " I can give you privileges and fiefs, but I cannot make you noble."

**The highest title :**

" He who is illuminated by the Holy Spirit is ennobled with the sovereign and highest nobility." (10).

**Nature's noblemen :**

The noble Italian Arnigio shows how truly generous and heroic peasants and men of the lowest rank of life may become. " The glorious nativity of the Redeemer of the world," he observes, " was revealed to shepherds, as to men pure, just, and vigilant. When our adorable Saviour was to be born blessed Mary and the devout Joseph were so little possessed of worldly grandeur that the stable of an inn was their only place of refuge." " For, mark," says a holy man, " the evangelists do not say that there was no room in the inn, but there was no room for them." Oh, what a noble school is poverty ! What a temple of sovereign honour !

**Right pride of birth :**

Pope Urban IV. was so little ashamed of being the son of a shoemaker that he ordered the pulpit of the church of St. Urban at Troyes, his native city, to be adorned on great festivals with tapestry representing his father's stall.

**Titled scoundrelism :**

There is even an example of legislation on the principle of the romances which places Chivalry before nobility; for the state of Pistoja, in the thirteenth century, ennobled men as a punishment for their crimes.

**Religion ennobles all :**

It is the sublime faith and the holy discipline of the Catholic Church which can enable the soul of man to gain the highest degree of elevation of which it is capable in its present state of exile. It is religion which can impart real magnanimity and gentleness to the lower classes, so as to make the most poor and obscure of men susceptible of all the generous and lofty sentiments which belong to true nobility.

In the little book entitled " Recollections of St. Acheul " there is an account of the life and death of a young student named Jean-Baptiste Carette. His parents were in such abject poverty that their son, having attracted the attention of a worthy priest, had been supported solely by the alms of charitable Christians. At their expense he was sent to the college of the Jesuits, about which the ' 'Recollections " were written. Here he manifested, during his short but brilliant career, for he died in his eighteenth year, not only the highest talents but a certain nobleness and purity of sentiments, which, adds the writer, " are not always found among those of the highest social standing." It was the custom at this college for the students to pass one day in the country every month during the summer season ; and Carette would employ these days in visiting his parents in their poor cottage. It was on one of these occasions that he was suddenly seized with the illness which removed him from the world. As soon as the news arrived at the college of his being unable to return, the Director of the Congregation of the Holy Angels, of which he was a member, hastened to visit him. He found him in

B

a miserable cabin, lying upon some straw which was spread upon some loose planks supported by stones. The pious youth, who remarked the Director's affliction on beholding him in such a state, said to him : " O Father, how good it is to submit to the Will of God ! " The holy man, having heard that he had already received the last sacraments, hastened back to the college to procure something which might relieve his suffering. But he did not return in time to find him alive. He had departed, repeating the words : " Gloria in excelsis Deo." Here we see in what a low and obscure condition of life nobleness and purity of sentiment may be found ; for there is no height and delicacy of honour, no refinement of sentiment, in fact, no perfection of Chivalry, which does not of necessity accompany such piety as this.

**Helmet above crown :**
But, while all men might aspire to the praise of noble Chivalry, its distinctions, which were nothing but those of nature, were esteemed of such surpassing dignity that even kings considered themselves as deriving their chief glory from possessing them. Witness the answer which Charles VI. of France made to his father when he was offered the choice between a crown of gold and a helmet as the emblem of that Chivalry which was the object of his admiration : " Monseigneur," exclaimed the young prince, with energy, " give me the helmet and keep your crown."

**Gentleman noblest title :**
The king was not the sole fountain of honour, for every simple knight could confer knighthood. Thus the chronicle of St. Denis relates that when Philippe, son of Philippe le Bel, at the Feast of Pentecost knighted his three sons, Louis, Philippe and Charles, these princes immediately conferred knighthood upon four hundred other youths. The dignity of a knight-banneret was hereditary. The degrees of nobility were not to interfere with its fundamental principle that one gentleman cannot be more gentle than another. Baldus says that an emperor or king is not more noble than a simple gentleman. Thus Francis I. writing to the Emperor Charles V. signed himself first gentleman of France ; and Henry IV. of

France used to say that his quality as a gentleman was the noblest title that he possessed. As an old writer says: " This was the general title throughout the world, so that nothing more idle can be thought of than for a particular prince to erect a new degree of blood above this title which is universal in all nations."

**Rank respected by poor :**

It is true what St. Francis de Sales said,(11) that " noble souls do not amuse themselves with this mess of trifles, rank, honour, salutations : they have other things to do : these things belong to slothful souls." Yet it is no less certain that the poor people who have the chivalry of nature in them always are inclined to respect nobility of birth in others. At least they are the last to declaim against it, because they know that it is not worth even a thought when divested of the spirit of Chivalry, and that where that Chivalry exists nobility of rank cannot interfere with the attainment of any object which can be dear to a noble heart. On the other hand demagogue nobles are the most decided enemies of freedom. In free states it is almost always such men that establish a tyranny.

**Politics not chivalrous :**

What a contrast to the mind of Chivalry is presented not only in the conduct but even in the orations of most public men ! How can this be accounted for ? The Roman philosopher Cicero supplies the best answer, in alluding to the vanity of Demosthenes : " That is to say he had learned to speak much amongst others but not to speak much with himself."

**Goodness of heart essential :**

Always in alliance with these sentiments was a disinclination to teach men that all persons should feel themselves destined for a political life. Aristotle mentions a person who would not suffer his son to take part in public affairs, saying : " If you speak justly men will hate you, if unjustly, the gods." The great sages of old from Thales the Milesian down to Anaxagoras, men like Pittacus and Bias, as Socrates remarked to Hippias, kept aloof from public affairs. And, though there is evidence in the ancient chronicles, as M. de Barante observes, to show that in our heroic ages public opinion and the general

wish of subjects exercised an immense power, it is also certain
that the thoughts and conversation of chivalrous men were
but little occupied with politics, which Landor calls " that
sad refuge of restless minds averse to business and to study."
For in truth the prosperity of states depends more upon the
hearts than upon the minds of subjects, however ardent these
may be in the promotion of schemes for the common good.
Berkeley, who may probably be regarded as an authority
not altogether beneath the attention of " a thinking people,"
says on one occasion : " I question whether everyone can
frame a notion of the public good, much less judge of the
means to promote it."

### Religion above politics :

In Catholic times men believed that the spirit of Christianity
ought to be the spirit of government, that the defence of
virtue and holiness ought to be its object, and that the law
of God ought to be its rule. " If we wish to consider the end
of all civil government," says Bartolommeo Arnigio, " which
is no other than to live well according to the divine pleasure
in order that we may put ourselves on the road which leads
to God, there is no surer rule or more certain way than the
religion of Jesus Christ."

### Religion favours true freedom :

" Besides this," says Schlegel, " there always is in every
Christian system of rule a formal and acknowledged principle
of justice. And moreover the Christian philosophy and the
views of human life which proceed from it are much more
favourable than is the revolutionary spirit to true freedom in
the highest sense of the word. By this freedom we understand
the spiritual, intellectual, and inward freedom, which must
always precede that which is the outward and civil freedom.
For if this last mentioned freedom is to be fruitful it must
correspond with the sense of these words : ' If therefore the
Son shall make you free, you shall be free indeed (12) ; to
comprehend which it must be observed that the Son makes
no man free otherwise than he was Himself free, namely by
obedience and by making the full offering of Himself in obedience to his Father."

**The sceptre of justice :**

How could anyone refrain from tears of joy and veneration in beholding the affecting solemnities with which the Church consecrated Godfrey, that humble disciple of Jesus Christ, who refused to wear the emblem of royalty, addressing him as she did in the words of the established form : " Take this wand as the emblem of your sacred power, in order that you may be able to strengthen the weak, sustain those who are in danger of falling, correct the vicious, and direct the good in the ways of salvation. Take the sceptre as the rule of Divine equity which governs the good and punishes the wicked ; let it teach you to love justice and to detest iniquity." Who more worthy of such a charge than Godfrey who was " a very righteous man of great prudence and a great lover of God and of the Church's ministers "? In surpassing state he walked, majestic in aspect, yet courteous, and bearing a crown of thorns in memory of his Saviour. "He was more capable of receiving the royal honour than any of the others," says an ancient chronicle, " for his private servants could find no fault in him excepting that he used to remain too long in the church after Mass and that he used to study too much the holy Gospels and the lives of the Saints and of the ancient Fathers ; which blame those who were to elect him regarded as a proof of his virtue."

**Mob law :**

Cicero says that "it is most absurd to suppose that all things are just which are found in the laws and institutions of a state. If all the Athenians should take pleasure in having tyrannical laws we on that account ought to suppose that such laws are just ? There is no such power," he continues, " in the sentence and command of fools that by their vote the nature of things can be reversed."

**Revolutionary liberty :**

In the Middle Ages the iron hand of the civil power was not felt, as it has been lately in so many nations, in restraining men from availing themselves of those great resources for the promotion of piety and wisdom which are furnished by the Catholic Church. Some modern governments of Europe show their cruelty in not allowing men openly to profess obedience to the counsels which our Lord has left us in His Gospel. They show extreme jealousy in legislating even against the holy habits or forms of dress consecrated by religion and associated with every idea of goodness and self-devotion, of faith and of sublime sanctity. It would seem as if really they were afraid that a man upon leaving his house should ever meet with persons whose clothing would tell him that they had renounced the world and that their lives were consecrated to God, that their only business was to instruct the poor, to tend the sick, and to console the dying. These governments are oppressive in interfering to obstruct the private spiritual enjoyments of men and even the general happiness of subjects. At one time they prevent the Church from acquiring property for the benefit of the poor, at another they annul legacies made in her favour. With barbarous violence they suppress the religious orders and even confiscate all the goods of the clergy, in order to please Jews, fanatics, and selfish calculators, who despise the people while they pretend to be their friends. With ignorant and insane cunning modern rulers contrive means to undermine the power of that clergy who only are the enlightened and steady advocates of the interests of the poor, men to whom these very governments owe every truth, every good, everything beautiful and sublime that they possess, and to the paralyzing of whose efforts all the wants and difficulties which distress them ought to be ascribed. And so they persevere in the development of an infernal project to injure and destroy the One, Holy, Catholic, and Apostolic church, taking counsel together by day and by night against the Lord and against His Christ. All these things were in the Middle Ages absolutely unknown.

### Socratic and Christian counsels :

Without presuming to undervalue the resources of modern wisdom, we may ask leave to affirm that if a Socrates were to arise in these days and to be a Christian he would see that the whole foundation of social order, the whole theory of political science, all ideas of the origin, rule, and object of government, had been changed since the first establishment of Christian states. He would therefore propose many questions and require many short and precise answers before he would admit that men who hold the original Christian principles could consistently continue to advise or direct those rulers who would be sure to reject their advice. At the same time, as a Christian, he would be the last to deny that the duty of obeying rulers where man does not command things which go against God, remains the same as in the first age of Christianity. Where rash or ignorant practitioners are administering palliatives that are more dangerous to the life than to the disease of the patient a wise physician will not remain in a position of responsibility if he be convinced that his counsels are not to prevail.

### Chivalry's mortal enemies :

In conclusion, it will be enough to remember that no form of government is absolutely incompatible with the existence of the chivalrous spirit, excepting despotism and anarchy. Under every other system, whatever may become of rulers and their ministers, there is no time so miserable as to prevent a man being a true man. But when a military or legal despotism, the latter being the more extreme evil, is once suffered to prevail, the spirit of Chivalry must then withdraw from all view of the world. Otherwise, were it to form a close alliance with what would infallibly act as poison to its purity and as a weight upon and obstacle to its independence, its warmest friends would soon be obliged to confess that indeed its age was then past and that nothing remained but to throw over it the sanctity of death.

NOTE : It must be remembered that the preceding paragraphs were written about a century ago, so that allowance should be made for changes in the Church's discipline which have been made to meet the needs of our own day. In more recent times the Holy See has in some cases signified a desire that Catholics should take part in public affairs even under an infidel government. On the other hand in the reign of Pope Leo XIII. Catholics in Italy were not permitted to enter parliament. So from age to age, with surpassing wisdom and unfailing charity, the Apostolic See watches over the highest temporal and spiritual interests of mankind. Ed.

# The Book of Tancredus

# The Book of Tancredus

EROIC ARDOUR WAS IN TANCRED, the noblest champion of the first Crusade, accompanied by the greatest humanity and moderation in war. It is expressly recorded of him by historians that on the capture of Jerusalem he used his utmost efforts to stop the massacre. When we consider the trying circumstances in which this humanity was displayed we must conclude that the true devotion of the chivalrous character was found in Tancred. It is therefore under the majesty of that illustrious and hercio name that this second book is presented to the reader.

## Religious spirit of Chivalry :

On examining the memorials of our Christian Chivalry it will be interesting to remark how the service of God was considered as demanding a perfect and total devotion of mind and heart, of soul and body, how the Catholic faith was the very basis of the character which belonged to the knight, how piety was to be the rule and motive of his actions and the source of every virtue which his conduct was to display. The first precept which was pressed upon the mind of youth was the love of God. "The precepts of religion," says M. Ste. Palaye, who was certainly not a writer prejudiced in favour of Chivalry, "left at the bottom of the heart a kind of veneration for holy things, which sooner or later acquired the ascendancy." A love of the Christian faith became the very soul of Chivalry. Every one has heard of the generous exclamation of Clovis when he was first made acquainted with the Passion and Death of Christ : " Had I been present at the

head of my valiant Franks I would have revenged His injuries."
It was upon hearing of the flagellation of our Saviour with all
its horrible circumstances that the brave Crillon gave that
celebrated proof of feeling; for he rose suddenly from his
seat moved by an involuntary transport, and laying his hand
on his sword exclaimed in those well-known words which have
passed into a proverb: "Where wast thou brave Crillon?"
This may not indicate the clearness of their religious views,
but it certainly shows the sincerity and the affection of their
hearts. And here it will be of importance to mark that this
peculiar characteristic of chivalrous devotion, the love of God,
furnishes an evidence that the religion of our ancestors was
far less removed from the true spirit of Christianity than many
have too hastily concluded from an imperfect acquaintance
with history. It is the motive rather than the action which
is peculiar to the religion of Jesus Christ. Now the religion
of Chivalry was altogether the religion of motives and of the
heart. It was love, faith, hope, gratitude, joy, fidelity,
honour, mercy; it was a devotion of mind and strength, of the
whole man, of his soul and body, to the discharge of duty and
to the sacrifice of every selfish and dishonourable feeling that
was opposed to duty; it was to obey a commandment which
was in unison with all the elevated sentiments of nature and
calculated most effectually to develope every quality that
ought to be the object of esteem and reverence. The knights
of old had neither the inclination nor the ingenuity to determine
the minimum of love which was compatible with the faith of
Christ. They were not like men who think it enough if they
love God at any time before death or on the festivals, or if
they keep the commandments and do not hate God, or who
imagine that this burdensome obligation of loving Him was
part of the Mosaic law which is dispensed with by the religion
of nature and the Gospel. They had not learned to reason
with the sophist of old, saying that religion "is a gracious
and an excellent thing when moderately pursued in youth;
but if afterwards it be loved over much it is the ruin of men."
They had not subsided into that state of profound indifference
to the truths of religion which the eloquent Massillon has
compared to the condition of Lazarus when the disciples
said: "Lord, if he sleep, he shall do well;" undeceived as

they were when Jesus said to them plainly : " Lazarus is
dead."(13). But their affections were warm, their gratitude
was sincere ; and, though their understanding as to the doctrines of religion might sometimes fail them, their hearts did
not. They were thankful under every circumstance of life ;
and, in the words of the prophet of old, it was their boast :
" 17. For the fig-tree shall not blossom : and there shall be
no spring in the vines. The labour of the olive-tree shall
fail : and the fields shall yield no food : the flock shall be cut
off from the fold, and there shall be no herd in the stalls.
18. But I will rejoice in the Lord : and I will joy in God my
Jesus."(14).

They were slain in battle, they were cut off in the flower
of their youth, they were shut up in dark prisons, deprived
of the light of the sun and of the solace of friendship ; yet
they could exult in the words of the Psalm : "25. For what have
I in heaven ? and besides Thee what do I desire upon earth ?
26. For thee my flesh and my heart hath fainted away :
Thou art the God of my heart, and the God that is my portion
for ever."(15). "Thenne," said Bors, " hit is more than yere
and an half that I ne lay ten tymes, where men dwelled, but
in wylde forestes and in mountains, but God was ever my
comforte." St. Louis, having been baptized in the castle at
Poissy, would bear that name and be called Louis of Poissy ;
and thus he signed his letters and despatches, esteeming this
title more glorious than that of King of France. And St.
Augustine, speaking of the Emperor Theodosius, says that
" He accounted himself more happy in being a member of
the Church than in being emperor of the world."(16). Observe
the exact and perfect loyalty with which God was served.
After the captivity of the King Saint Louis, when the treaty
was concluded according to which he was to be liberated,
the Saracens prescribed an oath which the King was to use in
swearing to fulfil the conditions. The form was as follows :
" That in case he did not hold to the things promised he should
be held to be forsworn, like to a Christian who has renounced
God, His baptism, and His law, and who, out of contempt for
God, spits on the Cross and breaks it to pieces under his feet."
" When the King," says Joinville, " heard this oath he said :
" I will not do it." In vain did his friends and enemies unite

against this resolution. He was reminded that it would cause not only his own death but also that of all his friends. " I love you," said he to the lords and prelates who remonstrated with him, " I love you as my brothers ; I love myself also ; but God forbid, whatever may come out of it, that such words should ever come from the mouth of a King of France. For you," he added in addressing the Saracen ministers, " go tell your masters that they can do as they will in this matter ; that I prefer immensely to die a good Christian than to live an object of anger to God, to His Mother, and to His Saints." The Emirs, distracted with rage and disappointment, rushed into his tent with their swords drawn crying out : "You are our prisoner and yet you treat us as if we were in irons; there is no middle way ; either death or the oath as we have drawn it." " God has made you masters of my body," replied the invincible Louis, " but my soul is in His hands ; you have no power over my soul." The King prevailed, and the infidels relinquished their resolution of requiring that the oath should be taken in the terms above mentioned.

Gauthier de Brienne, being made prisoner by the infidels at the battle of Gaza, was led by them before Jaffa, which they hoped to enter by a cruel stratagem. He was fastened to a cross and exposed to the view of the garrison, and threatened with death if resistance continued ; but he exhorted the garrison to hold out to the last. " It is your duty," he cried, to defend a Christian city ; it is mine to die for you and for Jesus Christ." After the fatal battle in Hungary, when the Turks had defeated the Christian army and had taken prisoners the valiant troop of French knights led by the Maréschal de Boucicaut and the Comte de Nevers, those brave and noble gentlemen were brought before Bayazid who received them in his tent. " It was a very piteous sight," says the old historian, " to see these noble gentlemen in the bloom of their early youth, of blood so high, and connected with that of the noble line royal of France, brought tightly bound with cords, all disarmed, in their little jackets, by those dogs of Saracens, ugly and horrible, who held them roughly in the presence of that tyrant enemy of the faith who was sitting there." All but the Comte de Nevers and the Maréschal de Boucicaut were led out to die like martyrs.

They were horribly cut with great knives on the head and breast and shoulders, and so were all butchered in cold blood. To be thus faithful to God was the constant lesson impressed upon youth: "Let Jesus also," says St. Bernard, "be ever in thy heart, and never let the image of the Crucified depart from thy mind." (17). Guilhem des Amalrics, a gentleman of Provence, begins one of his poems with a prayer: "God of my hope, my strength and only virtue, grant that I may never be opposed to thy pure and holy law, especially in times of danger, when a tempting enemy shall counsel me to forsake virtue." Gilles de Rome says in his *Mirror* that the knight or prince "ought to consider all his works or actions, and all his affections, intentions, and meditations, to the end that there may be nothing hidden which offends or angers the Divine Majesty." And King Perceforest in the romance says to his knights that he learned from Pergamon the ancient hermit that God deserves our love "on account of the love which He has for us, and not on account of any necessity which he has of us." It appeared on the trial of the Duc d'Alençon in the reign of Charles VII. that this nobleman had sent a servant to Italy to ask a certain celebrated hermit how he should act to gain the good graces of the King. The holy man gave this answer: "Let the Duc d'Alençon first of all gain the good grace of God, and then he will have that of all the world." Adam Davy had reason therefore to say:

> How gode men in olde tyme
> Loveden God almight
> That weren riche, of grete valoure,
> Kynges sonnes and emperoure,
> Of bodies strong and light.

This was the first precept of chivalrous education. The *Instruction d'un jeune Prince* by the celebrated George Chatelain, Counsellor of Philippe le Bon and Charles le Hardi of Burgundy, is divided into eight books. The first inculcates the love of God, the second the love of a ruler for his people, the third the love of justice, the fourth the good choice of ministers, the fifth the punishment of the guilty, the sixth the folly of unjust wars, the seventh is on finance and economy, the eighth on Chivalry.

## Maxims of Christian Chivalry

**A roll of honour :**

In the romance of the *White King* Maximilian is placed by his father under " a highly learned master, of virtuous, spiritual life, who instructs him in Latin, from whom he learns discipline and fear of God." " The true point of honour," says La Colombière in his *Theatre d' Honneur et de Chevalerie*, " on which our renown must depend, is to be a good man, and that is the true nature of honour. As for that honour which is acquired, it consists likewise in loving and fearing God, and in not imagining anything to be honour which is not to His honour ; and this is the commencement of all wisdom. This honour it is which leads a man to serve his king faithfully, to obey the laws, to fight bravely for his king and for his country, to follow the truth, reason, justice and equity, to love and assist his neighbour, to protect widows and orphans, to succour the poor and oppressed, to obey rulers, whether ecclesiastical or military or civil, and in all his actions to manifest that probity, that generosity, that virtue, the price and recompense of which is true honour. It is useless to seek the precise sense of honour anywhere else. And if we wish to rise still higher to heights above these precepts we must imitate Jesus Christ our Saviour in forgiving our enemies ; and then we shall possess not only the true temporal honour but also that which is heavenly and eternal." Such is the doctrine also of that great work *La Toison d'Or* composed by the Bishop of Tournay, chancellor of the Order of the Golden Fleece, dedicated to the high and mighty prince Charles Duke of Burgundy, containing a vast multitude of examples of chivalrous virtue, of magnanimity, confidence in other men, justice, innocence, friendship, pity, humility, obedience, discretion, hospitality, alms, liberality, truth, and faith. This great work was drawn up for the instruction of the knights of that illustrious Order.

The Bishop, indeed, speaks too much of Jason and of the virtue of the " young princes and noble cavaliers of Greece, whom Stacius the poet, on account of the worth of their prowess and valour, calls demi-gods," since Philip the Good declared that the Golden Fleece was suggested to him by Gideon and not by Jason, " who had broken his faith." In a similar spirit the great Alcuin composed his *Treatise on*

*Virtue and Vice* for the instruction of Count Gui, a noble warrior. Likewise the Abbot Smaragdus in the ninth century composed his *Via Regia* for teaching the truths of salvation to princes. Another book written with this view is the *Songe du Vieux Pèlerin* by Philippe de Maizières, who, after being secretary to Pope Gregory XI., then chancellor to the King of Cyprus, and intimate counsellor of King Charles V. of France, retired to the monastery of the Celestines at Paris, where he died at the end of the fourteenth century.

The *Livre du Chevalier de la Tour*, abounding with religious instruction, was written by the Seigneur de la Tour Landry of an ancient and illustrious house in Anjou and Maine. "The royal and noble dignity," says Gilles de Rome in his *Mirror of Chivalrous Virtue* "arises from the fear of God." He even goes so far as to say : "Worldly honour is not much to be desired, nay it is to be despised ; but the honour which ought to be cared for is the honour due to the soul, through which every good man takes great care to guard his own soul, recognizing in it the image of God through its special dignity, purchased as that soul is by the redemption, being the fruit of the atonement. And may we be able to arrive at meriting the reward of this faith by great earnestness in prayer, in sighs, in groans, and in tears, and by crying to God without ceasing." Children he says, should be taught what needs to be known about the Sacraments of the Church and to love God ; and they should be instructed in all things which belong to faith. And this should be done "before they have received into their thoughts any contrary impression of worldliness." To instruct youths in these principles there was also a book *De nobilitate Christiana* by the Portugese Bishop of Sylves in the Algarves, a treatise *De Ingenuis Moribus*, by Peter Paul Vergerio, who flourished at Padua towards the close of the fourteenth century, which treatise became so famous that public lectures upon it were given in the schools ; and there was the *Dialogue on Nobility* by Tasso. All these books will show that the fear and love of God formed the basis of Chivalry. Indeed, the distinction which Joinville has recorded between the "preuhomme" (valiant man) and the "preudhomme" (righteous man) will prove in a striking manner that in the opinion of the chivalrous age

c

a deep sense of religion was essential to a true knight.   Joinville is describing the character of Hugues Duc de Burgoigne :
" He was a very good knight with his hand and chivalrous.
But he was never reckoned as a good man in his relations
either to God or to the world.   And this appeared clearly
in his acts before mentioned.   And of him the great King
Philippe said, when he learned that Count John of Chalons
had a son born to whom the name of Hugues was given :
' May God will to make him a valiant man and a righteous
man.   For there is a great difference,' he said, ' between a
valiant man and a righteous man ;' and he said that many
cavaliers there were amongst the Christians and amongst the
Saracens who were valiant enough and yet not righteous.
For they had no fear or love whatever towards God.   And
he said that God gave a great grace to a knight when he
possessed this good gift that through his deeds he was called
a valiant man and a righteous man.   But he of whom we
have just spoken could rightly he called a valiant man only,
for he was brave and bold so far as the body was concerned,
but not in his soul.   For he did not fear to commit sin or
to behave ill towards God."   The Bishop of Auxerre, in his
funeral oration on Du Guesclin, as recorded by the monk of
St. Denys the historian of Charles VI. of France, proves by
a reference to the duties of Chivalry that even the title of
" preux " (valiant) did not belong to any but such as were
religious as well as brave, and that even these must not aspire
to it in their lifetime.   Therefore, the heralds cried : " Honour
to the sons of the valiant ;" " for," says Monstrelet, " no
knight can be judged valiant till after he has passed away."
As a natural consequence the defence of religion became the
office and the pride of the ancient nobility.   " The duty of
a knight," says a work quoted by Ste. Palaye, " is to maintain
the Catholic faith ;  and the author of this work presents
his readers with a passage from Eustache Deschamps (18) :

> Chevaliers en ce monde cy
> Ne peuvent vivre sans soucy ı
> Ils doivent le peuple défendre
> Et leur sang pour la foi espandre.

Perfectly conformed to these injunctions was the conduct

34

of the ancient nobility. The Cross of Christ was no sooner lifted up as the standard under which the defenders of the faith were to rally than all Europe was united in a band of brothers to testify love for the Saviour of mankind. Germany, France, and England, poured forth the flower of their youth and nobility, men who were led by no base interest or selfish expectation but who went with single hearts, renouncing the dearest blessings of their country and station, to defend the cause which was dear to them and to protect from insult and wrong the persecuted servants of their Saviour.

Godfrey of Bouillon, Robert Count of Flanders " the Sword and Lance of the Christians," Robert Duke of Normandy, son of William the Conqueror, who hung up as a trophy the standard and sword of the Sultan in the vault of the Holy Sepulchre, and who refused to be king, pronouncing Godfrey more worthy. Hugues de Saint Paul, Conon de Montaigu, Raimond I. Viscount of Turenne, Gaston de Foix, Geoffroi de la Tour who slew the enormous serpent and delivered the lion, Raimond Count of Toulouse, Duke of Narbonne, and Marquis of Provence, whose long white hair floating over his armour, joined with the enthusiasm of youth, made him appear the father and the model of the Paladins, he who had fought under the banner of the Cid and been conqueror over the Moors in Spain, the first to take the cross and to rouse the youth of Languedoc and Provence, the mightiest of the French princes, and both the Achilles and the Nestor of the Crusaders, Hugh the great, the hero of Antioch, Stephen Count of Chartres and Blois who possessed as many towns as there are days in the year, Tancred of Sicily, " who in the wars of the Lord merited the title of the highest wisdom in youth," and of whom another historian says that he had " a mind which despised money," Baldwin and Eustache, Josselin de Courtenay, Bohemund prince of Taranto, Gerard founder of the hospital of St. John at Jerusalem, Raimond Dupuy the first military grandmaster, Hugues de Payens founder of the Templars, that renowned Order " whose virtues and battles and glorious triumphs over the enemies of Christ all the Church of the Saints will narrate," the lion-hearted Richard of England, St. Louis the hero of France and the honour of the world, Alphonsus Count of Poitiers, Robert of

Artois, Peter Count of Brittany, Hugh Duke of Burgundy, Dampierre Count of Flanders, Hugh de Lusignan Count of la Marche, William Longsword Earl of Salisbury, the Counts of Bar, Dreux, Soissons, Rethel, Vendome, Montfort, Foulques Count of Anjou, Erard and Gautier de Brienne, the Joinvilles, the Châtillons, the Coucys, who were the light and glory of Europe, these with others among the bravest and most noble of their generation, " whose names are committed to the memory of God only," hastened to proclaim to the world by their deeds and devotion that the Saviour of mankind was dear to them. What instances of sincerity and faith do these annals furnish ! Witness the heroism of Reynaud de Châtillon who refused life upon conditions of apostasy and was beheaded by the hand of Saladin. Witness also that of the crowd of knights of the two Orders of the Temple and of St. John who suffered themselves to be massacred in prison by order of the same infidel rather than renounce Jesus Christ. Vertot relates that the Chevalier de Temericourt, after gallantly defeating the Turkish fleet, was forced by a tempest upon the coast of Barbary where he was taken prisoner. He was led to Tripoli and thence to Adrianople where he was presented to Mahomet III. who asked if he was the man who had fought five of his great ships. " It was I," answered the knight. " Of what nation are you ?" demanded the Sultan. " French," said Temericourt. " Then you are a deserter," continued Mahomet, " for there is a solemn league between me and the King of France." " I am French," said Temericourt, " but in addition to belonging to that nation I am also a knight of Malta, a profession which binds me to risk my life in fighting against all the enemies of the Christian name." He was conducted to prison, where he was at first well treated. Every expedient was tried to prevail upon a youth of twenty-two years to renounce his religion. He was offered a princess of the blood in marriage and the office of grand admiral. But all in vain. The Sultan became irritated ; the prisoner was thrown into a dungeon where he was beaten with rods and tortured ; but this generous confessor of Jesus Christ did only invoke His Name and pray for His grace. Finally he was beheaded by command of the Sultan. The Emperor David Comnenus was taken at the sur-

36

render of Trebizond whence he was conducted by Mahomet to Constantinople. Here new terms were forced upon him, either to renounce the faith or to die. The Greek Emperor, who had consented to surrender his empire to the conqueror, now recalling the ancient sentiments of religion, which ambition had suppressed, preferred death to apostasy ; and he had the consolation to witness seven of his sons possessed of the same fidelity.

The monk Guibert speaks of one, among those knights who gladly chose death rather than deny their faith, " whom," he says, " I have known from his boyhood and seen grow up to manhood, we being both from the same town and our parents being also familiar with each other. He was of noble birth and distinguished for virtue. Being taken by the infidels and required to renounce the faith of Christ he prevailed on them to wait till the Good Friday which was then approaching. When the day arrived he astonished them by saying with noble firmness that he was ready to be put to death : ' I will render up my life to Him Who has on this day laid down His own life for the salvation of all men.' His head was cut off with one blow of a scimitar."

When the day of the battle of Antioch arrived Hugh the Great was entreated by his friends and vassals to remain on his bed to which he had been confined by a burning fever. " No, no," cried he, " I will not wait in cowardly repose for a shameful death ; it is amongst you brave companions in arms that I wish to die this day with glory for Jesus Christ." The conduct of the brave Maréschal Gaspard de Vallier, governor of Tripoli is well known. That of the Chevalier Abel de Bricliers de la Gardampe, during the memorable siege of Malta, was also most noble. Having received a mortal wound he would not permit his comrades to remove him from the spot, saying : " Count me no more amongst the number of the living ; your care will be better employed in defending our other brothers." He crawled into the chapel of the castle and expired at the foot of the altar in recommending his soul to God. On the evening of the 23rd of June the Turks resolved to make the assault the following morning, and the knights who defended the fort, having lost all hope of succour, received the Blessed Sacrament in the dead of the night. They then embraced one another and went to their respective posts to fulfil their last duty by delivering up their souls to God. The wounded were carried to the breach in chairs, where they sat with their swords grasped with both hands. They were killed to a man ; and Mustapha ordered their dead bodies, after being cut into crosses and fastened to boards, to be cast into the sea.

### The Holy City :

Who can read the account which William of Tyre gives of the entrance of the Crusaders into Jerusalem without emotion ? " Having laid aside their arms, in the spirit of humility and with a contrite mind, with bare feet and washed hands, with all splendid habits laid aside, with groans and tears, they began to go round devoutly, and to kiss with deep sighs the venerable places which the Saviour wished to render illustrious and to sanctify by His presence. It was a grateful sight and full of spiritual joy to behold with what devotion, with what a pious fervour of desire, the faithful people approached the holy places, with what exaltation of mind and spiritual joy they kissed the memorials of our Lord's earthly mission. Everywhere were tears and sighs, not such as grief and anxiety excite but such as fervent piety and the consummate joy of the interior man are accustomed to offer up as a holocaust to the Lord. Immediately they began to contend earnestly amongst themselves, desiring to conquer in works of piety, having the divine grace before their eyes."

### Faithful unto death :

Josselin de Courtenay while inspecting the demolition of a certain tower near Aleppo was crushed by the falling of part of the building so as to be confined to his bed for a long time. At length the Sultan of Iconium came and laid siege to a camp belonging to Josselin called Croison. Josselin called his son and charged him to collect a force sufficient to compel the Sultan to abandon the siege. The son, being of little courage, declared that he was unequal to the task of resisting the Sultan. Then the dying warrior understood what sort of a person was about to succeed him. He ordered himself to be carried in his bed against the Turks. While he was yet on the way the news reached him that the Sultan, hearing of his resolution to be carried in his bed to meet him, had raised the siege and hastily departed. Josselin, causing his litter to be laid on the ground and raising up his hands and eyes towards heaven, with a pious heart returned great thanks to God for all the honour and benefits which he had received during his life, and especially that lying half dead on his bed he had terrified the potent enemy of the Christian name. For he knew that all these things had been brought about only by the divine goodness and care. And with such words he rendered up his soul to God.

### A religious hero :

Let us draw nearer and view the persons and countenances and admire the virtue of the crusading princes. And first let us speak of Tancred : " Neither did his ancestral riches move him to luxury," says Radulphus, " nor the power of his relations to pride. When young he excelled other youths in agility and the exercise of arms, and old men in gravity of manners, to both affording an excellent example of virtue. A sedulous hearer of the precepts of God, he studied with diligence both to remember what he had heard and, as far as possible, to fulfil what he remembered ; and so he would detract from the merit of no one even when this led to himself being disparaged. The very herald of an enemy's virtue, he used to say : ' An enemy should receive blows not back-biting.' He spoke never about himself, but he thirsted insatiably to merit to be the object of other men's praise. He preferred vigils to sleep, labour to rest, hunger to fulness, study to ease, and all things necessary to superfluities."

" When this religious hero first saw Jerusalem from an eminence he knelt down with bare knees upon the earth and raised his heart to heaven the image of which he seemed to behold. Then rising up he left his soldiers and alone he ascended the Mount of Olives and looked again upon the holy city. But oftener he turned his eyes towards Calvary and the church of our Lord's Sepulchre, a spectacle indeed more distant, but attainable to his eagerness. With sighs and tears he would have offered an age as the price of that one day. But happier still would he have been had he been able to kiss

39

the vestiges on Calvary." "Happy was the simple old woman who was found by Tancred, exhausted as she was with hunger and about to wade across a rapid torrent, for immediately there was meat for the hungry and a horse instead of a ship, a knight, yea, Tancred himself, instead of a rower, for her who was about to cross over." "There was but one mind in the whole army. Oh, who amongst the children of men was equal to thee, Tancred ? Who less inclined to sloth, to ease, to fear, to pride, or to luxury ? Who more ready when called ? who more willing ? who more placable when offended ? Blessed be God Who hath reserved thee to be the guard of His people ; and thou art blessed who canst defend that people with thy arm. To be with Tancred was to be in safety : to be without him in the army was like not being with the army."

**Rich in virtues :**
   Godfrey of Bouillon is thus described : " He was rich in virtues, in those that are secular and in those that are divine, bountiful to the poor, merciful to those who were in fault, distinguished by humility, humanity, soberness, justice, chastity. You would have thought him rather the light of monks than the general of soldiers. Nevertheless, he was equally excellent in secular virtues, in battle, and in the conduct of an army." By the monk Robert, Godfrey is thus described : " Elegant he was in countenance, commanding in stature, sweet in speech, distinguished in manners, and mild to such an extent that he presented the figure rather of a monk than of a soldier. Nevertheless, this man, when he felt that the foe was near and the battle close at hand, braced up his soul with daring mind, and furious as a lion he feared no one's attack ; and what coat of mail or shield could stand against his sword's assault ?" All said of him : " He rather honoured the kingly dignity than was honoured by it." William of Tyre thus describes him : " He had his origin from illustrious and religious ancestors. His father was the Lord Eustachius the illustrious and magnificent Count of Boulogne and Lens whose deeds were many and memorable and whose memory to this day, among the old people of the neighbouring countries, is with a blessing, and devoutly reverenced as that

40

of a religious man fearing God. His mother was distinguished among the noble matrons of the West as well for excellence of virtues as for the brightest title of nobility. Godfrey was a religious man, clement, pious, and fearing God, just, departing from all evil, grave, and firm in word, despising the vanities of the age, which in one of his time of life, especially when following the military profession, is a rare virtue, assiduous in prayer and in works of piety, remarkable for liberality, gracious with affability, kind and merciful, in all his ways commendable, and pleasing to God. He was of lofty stature yet so as to be less tall than the very tallest although higher than the generality, robust beyond all example, firmly built, with a manly chest, with a most dignified and beautiful countenance, with his hair and beard inclining to auburn. According to the judgment of all men he was unrivalled in the use of arms and in military exercise." His refusing to wear a crown is finely illustrative of his humble piety. " Being moved," says William of Tyre, " by humility he was unwilling to be distinguished by a golden crown, after the manner of Kings, in the holy city, exhibiting in this way great reverence, because the Restorer of the human race, in that very spot, and even on the wood of the Cross, chose for our salvation to wear a crown of thorns. Hence it is that some, incapable of distinguishing merit, are unwilling to reckon him in the catalogue of kings, looking more to what is borne outwardly on the body than to what is pleasing to God in the soul. But in our judgment he seems not only a king but the best of kings, the light and the model of all others."

**King, hero and saint :**
Joinville bears testimony to the personal heroism of St. Louis : " Be sure that the good King on this day achieved the greatest feats of arms which I have ever seen performed in any battle of all those in which I have ever been. And they say that if it were not for his personal presence on that day we should have been all lost and destroyed. But I believe that the valour and power which he usually possessed were half doubled on that occasion through the power of God. For he cast himself into the midst in whatever place he saw his people hard pressed and dealt great mace and sword

strokes in marvellous fashion. And one day the Sire de Courtenay and Messire Jehan de Salenay related to me that six Turks on that day drew near to the King and seized hold of the rein of his horse and were dragging him away by force. But the brave King put forth all his strength and smote these Turks with such great courage that he alone saved himself."

### The Crusades justified :

The defence of a military expedition to invade the country of the infidels presents another question. In this respect however, the Crusades are easily justified on every principle of justice and policy. Xenophon relates that all the world admired the spirit and policy of Agesilaus in determining to meet the barbarians on their own territory rather than to wait till they had invaded Greece, when he would have had to meet them on the defensive. Precisely similar was the case of the Crusades. When St. Bernard and the Popes called upon the princes of Christendom to take the Cross it was to save Europe and to prevent the Crescent from dispossessing the Cross. There is not a point of history more clearly established than is this, by the concurrent testimony of all real historians. Hence has the memory of the Crusades been ever dear to all great men who loved Christianity. Thus Dante sees the Cross placed in the planet Mars to denote the glory of those who fought in the Crusades. Raumer even says that for importance and efficacy nothing can be compared to the victory of Charles Martel but that of the Greeks of old over the Persians. How grateful should Christians feel to the Roman Pontiffs for their watchful solicitude ! That illustrious Pope Pius II. had reason when he said in his celebrated speech in 1463, which was repeatedly interrupted by the tears of the assembly, that the following of the Cross would prove the sincerity of the devotion of his hearers. " Now let your faith, your religion, your piety, be brought to the light. If it be a true and not a feigned charity follow Us. We will set you an example that you may do what We are about to perform. Yes, We will imitate Our Master and Lord Jesus Christ the loving and holy Shepherd Who did not fear to lay down His life for His sheep. We will lay down Our life for Our flock, since in no other way can We bear assistance to the Christian religion, that it be not trodden down by the Turkish men. We will mount the ship, though old and broken down with sickness. ' And what can *you* do in war ? ' some one will say. 'An old man, a priest, oppressed with a thousand maladies, will you go into battle ? ' We will imitate the holy father Moses, We will stand on the lofty prow or on the top of some mountain, having the divine Eucharist before Our eyes, that is Our Lord Jesus Christ, and We will implore from Him salvation and victory for Our soldiers in the fight. A contrite and humbled heart the Lord will not despise. The kingdom of the Church cannot be preserved unless We imitate Our predecessors who maintained that kingdom. Nor is it enough to be confessors, to preach to the people, to thunder against vices, to exalt virtue to heaven : We must rise to the level of those who have offered up their bodies for the testament of the Lord. For Our God We leave Our own See and the Roman Church, and We devote to the cause of piety these grey hairs and this weak body. He will not be unmindful of Us. If He will not grant Us a return to Our home He will grant an entrance to heaven, and He will preserve His Primal See and His reproachless Spouse."

### What makes a true Knight ?

In the admirable book of chivalrous instruction by Gilles de Rome entitled *The Mirror* it is laid down how the prince, baron, or knight, should be grounded in the truths of faith, steadfast in faith, firm in hope, strong in the love of God, perfect in the fear of God. " He ought to be fervent in prayer for the love of Jesus Christ, to have reverence and devotion towards the Church, to be humble in himself, to have reasonable knowledge, to be stable in perseverance and constant in execution, honest in conversation, secret in consultation, discreet in speech, courteous in receiving strangers, liberal in gifts, magnificent and noble in actions, magnanimous in enterprises, continent in purity, abstinent in sobriety, amiable in all good qualities, incomparable in clemency and invincible in patience." " He must be founded in the Catholic faith, which is the source of all graces. That faith is the foundation of justice, it purifies us from our sins, it enlightens our thoughts, it reconciles us to God, and accompanies us amidst all the goods of nature."

### A Knight of Our Lady :

When the city of Granada was besieged a gigantic Moor had obtained possession of an ecclesiastical ornament whereon the " Ave Maria " was embroidered, and he paraded on the plain (vega) of Granada with it fixed to his horse's tail. This was enough to make boil the blood of Garcilaso, at that time a mere stripling. He challenged the Moor, slew him, and brought the trophy to the Christian camp. In reward for this gallant exploit the King of Aragon gave him leave to adopt the title De la Vega and to place the words " Ave Maria " on his ancestral shield.

### John Sobieski, King of Poland :

Too little is youth reminded of these great events. For the names of Charles Martel who saved Christendom under the walls of Poitiers, of Matthias Corvinus King of Hungary in the 15th century who had the glory of stopping Mahomet II. in the midst of his conquests, and perhaps of again saving Christendom, and of John Sobieski King of Poland who saved the house of Austria and probably the whole of Europe, should be associated with all the visions of greatness and glory. The Turks with an army of more than 200,000 men besieged Vienna. The Emperor Leopold after a narrow escape had fled to Passau, and Vienna the great bulwark of Christendom was in immediate danger of falling into the hands of the infidels. Then it was that the King and the chivalry of Poland hastened to save the Empire and Christianity. Leopold had previously injured Sobieski ; but on this occasion, like a brave true knight, the King thought of nothing but what he owed to an ally, to all Christendom, and to God Himself. With all possible expedition he advanced to the Danube at the head of not more than 76,000 men. He crossed the river at Tuln and ascended the mountains of Kahlenberg, whence on the 11th of September 1683, he and his army had their first view of Vienna. The city was half obscured by the volumes of smoke arising from the discharge of artillery, while the plain below presented the most magnificent but awful spectacle of the Turkish camp adorned with all that eastern pomp could display. The letters of Sobieski to his beloved queen convey a great idea of his piety and noble simplicity. Of this memorable expedition he relates on one occasion how he had assisted at High Mass in the Franciscan convent of Brünn. Again, after crossing the Danube, he says : " We passed yesterday in prayer. Father Marco d' Avieno, who has come from the Pope, gave us His benediction. We received the Blessed Sacrament from his hands. After Mass he gave us an address and asked us if we had confidence in God ? And on our unanimous answer that we had he made us repeat with him, ' Jesus Maria,' Jesus Maria !' He said Mass with the most profound devotion. He is truly a man of God." This scene, at which the Duke of Lorraine was present, took place on the 12th September two hours before sunrise in St. Leopold's chapel. The King served at Mass holding his arms stretched out in the form of a cross. Immediately after the whole army was put in motion to meet the enemy. The main body was commanded by the Electors of Bavaria and Saxony with Count Waldeck, the right wing by the King of Poland, and the left by Charles Duke of Lorraine. Mustapha and the whole Turkish army were put to flight in the utmost disorder and before night there was not a Turk to be seen. The conquerors found immense riches. Sobieski wrote to his queen that the Grand Vizier had made him his sole executor. The great standard that was found in the Vizier's tent, made of the hair of the sea-horse, wrought with a needle and embroidered with Arabic figures, was hung up by the order of the Emperor in the cathedral of St. Stephen, where I (Kenelm Digby) have seen it. The Christians lost but 600 men. Sobieski, the modest religious hero, entered Vienna amidst the tears and blessings of innumerable people. He went directly to the high altar in the church and joined in the solemn Te Deum which was sung, with his countenance turned towards the ground and with every expression of humility and gratitude. The Emperor, who returned to his capital on the 14th of September, treated his deliverer with haughtiness. The brave Sobieski, despising the ceremonial of courts, content to meet his Imperial Majesty on horseback, was satisfied when he had said : " I am glad to have rendered

Your Majesty this little service." He pursued the Ottoman army, fought many battles, and returned to Warsaw crowned with laurels. On the taking of Gran from the Turks he wrote to his queen in these words : " The great church in which St. Adalbert baptized King Stephen, the first Christian King of Hungary, had been converted into a mosque. A solemn Mass will be sung there shortly." Again, on the taking of Schetzin : " To-morrow the divine office is to be celebrated in the two mosques. Thus we have regained five churches in this year from the Paynims ; thanks to Almighty God." Again, describing the cruel treatment inflicted upon his brave army by the Hungarian Calvinists, though he had always declared that he made no war upon them but only upon the Turks, he writes thus : " They hunt us as if we were wolves. Many of our officers have had their horses shot in the midst of the camp, without our having given the smallest cause for such attacks. However, I take into consideration that there are in this city many peaceable innocent Catholics who would all perish if we made an assault." What battle of antiquity is more deserving of everlasting fame than that of Las Navas de Tolosa, which saved Spain and perhaps all Europe !

> Illustrious Spain !
> Alas, what various fortunes has she known !
> Yet ever did her sons her wrongs atone.

This memorable victory was obtained in the year 1212 on the ground between El Viso and Venta de Miranda near the Sierra Morena on the Puerto Real, as it was called from that day. The King of Navarre commanded the right wing of the Christian army, the King of Aragon the left ; Alfonso VIII. of Castile took the centre, as the post of most danger. Muhammed sat enthroned on a buckler, amidst a corps of reserve, holding the Koran in one hand and a sword in the other and surrounded by chains of iron. In consequence of the King of Navarre having burst his way through this iron barrier chains were borne quarterly in the shield of France.

### Nobility guardian of religion :

But it was not only to defend the Christian religion that Chivalry bound its sons. The great and powerful were to be examples of the influence of religion : they were to devote their riches and their grandeur to maintain its institutions and to exalt its glory.

This principle cannot be better expressed than in the words of the Count de Maistre, who, more perhaps than any other writer of this age, has imbibed the spirit of the Christian Chivalry. "True nobility," he says, "is the natural guardian of religion ; it is related to the priesthood and it never ceases to protect it." Appius Claudius cried out in the Roman Senate that religion was the affair of the patricians : "The sacrifices belong to the fathers ;" and Bourdaloue, twenty centuries later, said in a Christian pulpit : "Holiness to be eminent can find no foundation more suitable to itself than grandeur."

**Holiness of Knighthood :**

All the laws of Chivalry were dictated by this spirit. The first was : "To fear, honour, and serve God, to contend with all his strength for the faith, and rather to suffer a thousand deaths than to renounce Christianity." Then : "To support justice, to attend to the proper complaints of the weak, especially of widows, orphans and damoiselles, and, when necessity requires, to undertake their cause, saving always his own honour ; to fight for the right and common cause." This close connection between the defence of religion and of justice is shown in the admission made by Sismondi, namely, that during the civil wars between Lothair II. and Conrad III. the Guelfs were at once the defenders of the Church and of the privileges of the people. Again, in the old poem on the order of Chivalry, the virtues which are peculiarly to distinguish a knight are seven, of which the first three are, faith, hope, and charity. And Eustache Deschamps says : "You who desire to become knights must pursue a new course of life. Devoutly you must watch in prayer, avoid sins, pride, and idleness ; you must defend the Church, widows and orphans, and with noble boldness you must protect the people." In *L'Ordene de Chevalerie*, by Hugues de Tabarie, that is, by Hugues Chatelain de St. Omer, Comte de Tiberiade, we read that the squire who was to be made a knight was to be placed in a beautiful bed and to be addressed thus : Sire, this signifies (19) :

47

> C'on doit par sa chevalerie
> Conquerre lit en Paradis
> Ke Dieu otroie à ses amis.

He was to be dressed in white to signify :

> A se car netèment tenir
> Se il à Dieu velt parvenir.

Then he was to have a scarlet robe to signify :

> Que vostre sang deves espandre
> Et pour Sainte Eglise deffendre.

Then he was to put on black sandals to signify :

> La mort, et la terre ou girez
> Dont venistes, et ou irez.

Then he was to be bound with a white girdle to signify purity, then two gilt spurs were to be fastened on, to signify activity :

> Que vous ayez bien en corage
> De Dieu servir tout vostre éage.

Then he girded on the sword to show :

> K'il doit la povre gent garder,
> Ke li riches nel puist foler,
> Et le feble doit soustenir,
> Que li fors ne le puist honir,
> Ch' est oevre de misericorde.

Finally he was to be covered with a white garment to signify the purity with which we must clothe our soul against the day of judgment.

### Conferring of Knighthood :

Count William of Holland when elected King of the Romans in 1277 was knighted at Cologne. At this time he was only a squire, so it was necessary, according to the custom of creating the Christian Emperors, that he should be made a knight before he received the crown of the Empire at Aix-la-Chapelle. When everything was prepared in the church at Cologne, after Mass the Squire William was led by the King of Bohemia before the Cardinal, Father Caputzius, Legate of the Pope Innocent, when the King addressed the Cardinal in these words : " We place before your honoured Reverence, beloved father, this squire, humbly beseeching that in paternal kindness you would accept his desires that he may become worthy of associating among knights." Then the Cardinal said to the youth : " What is a knight according to the meaning of that word ? Whosoever desireth to obtain knighthood must be high-minded, open-hearted, generous, superior, and firm ; high-minded in adversity, open-hearted in his dealings, generous in honour, superior in courtesy, and firm in manly honesty. But before you make your vow take this yoke of the Order which you desire into mature consideration. These are the rules of Chivalry : 1st. Before all, with pious remembrance every day to hear the Mass of God's Passion. 2nd. To risk body and life boldly for the Catholic faith. 3rd. To protect Holy Church with her servants from every one who shall attack her. 4th. To search out widows and helpless orphans in their necessity. 5th. To avoid engaging in unjust wars. 6th. To refuse unreasonable rewards. 7th. To fight for the deliverance of innocence. 8th. To pursue warlike exercises only for the sake of perfecting warlike strength. 9th. To obey the Roman Emperor or his deputy with reverence in all temporal things. 10th. To hold inviolable the public good. 11th. In no way to alienate the feudal tenures of the Empire. 12th. And without reproach before God or man to live in the world. When you shall have faithfully attended to these laws of Chivalry, know that you shall obtain temporal honour on the earth, and, this life ended, eternal happiness in heaven." When the Cardinal had said this he placed the joined hands of the young warrior on the holy book of the Mass, out of which the gospel had been read, saying : " Wilt thou piously receive knighthood in the name of God, and fulfil, to the best of thy power, according to the letter, what has been taught ?" The squire answered : " I will." Thereupon the Cardinal gave him the following solemn instruction which the youth read aloud publicly : " I William, Count of Holland, knight and vassal of the holy Roman Empire, swear to observe the rules of knighthood in presence of my Lord Peter of the Golden Fleece, Cardinal Deacon, and Legate of the Apostolic See, by this Holy Gospel which I touch with my hands." Then the Cardinal said : "May this devout confession give thee pardon of thy sins !" This spoken, he gave the squire a blow on the neck and said : "For the honour of God Almighty I make you a knight, and do you take the obligation.

D

But remember how He was smitten in the presence of the High Priest Caiphas, how He was mocked by Pilate the governor, how He was beaten with scourges, crowned with thorns and arrayed in royal robe, how He was derided before King Herod, and how He, naked before all the people, was hanged upon the Cross. I counsel you to think upon His reproach, and I exhort you to take upon you his Cross." After this had taken place the new knight, amidst the sound of trumpets, beat of kettle-drums, and crash of musical instruments, ran three times against the son of the King of Bohemia to display his warlike exercise in battle. Then he held court for three days and maintained his honour before all the great by princely gifts.

### Religion in Knights :

In Froissart we read the description which the Portugese ambassadors gave of King John of Portugal to the Duke of Lancaster. "He is," said they, "a wyse and a dyscrete man, and fereth God, and loveth holy Churche, and exalteth it as moche as he may, and is often tymes in his oratory on his knees in herying of devyne servyce. He hath ordeyned that, for whatsoever busyness it be, none speke to hym till he be out of his oratory. And he is a grete clerke, and taketh lytlle hede of ony grete sermones, and especyally he wyll have justyce kept in all his royalme, and poore men maynteyned in theyr ryght." John of Salisbury describes the necessity and nature of the religious oath which every Norman knight took on his creation. He swore to "defend the Church, to attack the perfidious, to venerate the priesthood, to repel all injuries from the poor, to keep the country quiet, and to shed his blood, and, if necessary, to lose his life, for his brethren." Even the legendary institution of the Round Table is an example of this religious feeling, for the thirteen places were in memory of our Lord and His chosen Twelve, that of Judas remaining vacant. Romance says that the twelve places were successively filled during King Arthur's reign by fifty knights. The rules of the Order may be seen in the *Romance of Merlin*. Rodolph of Hapsburg may be cited as an illustrious example of this religious Chivalry. No family had ever a more honourable founder than his ; for Rodolph was beloved by the people of the surrounding country for his justice and his piety, his prudence and his courage. Schweitz begged him to be her governor, Zurich to be her general ; and when raised to the throne of the Empire he was still beloved by the country which gave him birth. When he was to be crowned at Aachen the imperial sceptre could not be found at the moment when he was to invest the assembled princes ; upon which, with admirable presence of mind, and in the true spirit of Chivalry, he seized the crucifix which stood on the altar and said aloud, " With this sceptre will I for the future govern."

### Last advice of Charlemagne :

We have another instance in the last advice of Charlemagne to his son as related by Theganus. " On the Sunday he put on the royal robe, placed his crown on his head, and assumed a purple habit. He then proceeded to the church which he had built from its foundation, and coming before the altar he ordered his golden crown and also that which he wore on his head to be placed upon it. After he had spent a long time in prayer together with his son he addressed him before all the assembly of pontiffs and nobles, admonishing him, in the first place, to love and fear Almighty God, to keep His precepts in all things, to provide for and defend from bad men the churches of God; then to honour priests as fathers, to love his people as sons. He told him that he should appoint faithful ministers who feared God and who held unjust gifts in abhorrence, that he should show himself at all times without reproach before God and all the people."

### Christian servants :

Gilles de Rome, in his *Mirror*, gives an admirable lesson to the great when he shows that noble princes and barons ought to consider their servants as their brethren ; for, he continues, " It is not said in Genesis that God gave man dominion over man, but servitude is the consequence of sin and of the fall." " It is a thing becoming thy prudence to live familiarly with thy servants ; they are somewhat more than mere serfs, they are men and servants and humble friends and fellow-serfs with thyself." The most base slavery is that of sin. "And through this it is clear that it is a thing possible that the serf be lord and the lord serf." A modern writer has well expressed the same idea thus : " Vice is the greatest of all Jacobins, the arch-leveller."

## A mother of good counsel :

The advice of Dame Terrail to her son the Chevalier Bayyard is another striking instance. The young page was already mounted on his little horse in the castle-court and accompanied by his good uncle the Bishop of Grenoble who was to conduct him to Chambéry. His father had bestowed his blessing and all the youth of the castle were taking affectionate leave of their companion. " The poor lady his mother was in a tower of the castle and she was tenderly weeping. For, joyous as she was because her son was on the point of making a start in life, yet a mother's love bade her weep. Nevertheless, after someone had come to say to her : ' Madame if you wish to come to see your son he is ready on horseback and prepared to set out,' the good gentlewoman came forth at the back of the tower and causing her son to come to her she spoke to him these words, ' Peter, my friend, you are going into the service of a gentle prince. As far as a mother can command her child I command you to observe three things; and if you fulfil them be assured that you will live with honour in this world and that God will bless you. The first is that you fear God, serve Him, and love Him, without ever offending Him, if that be possible. It is He Who has created us, in Whom we live, and by Whom we are preserved. It is by Him that we shall be saved. Without Him and without His grace we should never be able to perform the smallest good action. Be particular to pray to Him every day, both morning and evening, and He will assist you. The second is, that you be gentle and courteous towards the nobility, that you show neither haughtiness nor pride towards any person, that you be ready always to oblige every person, that you avoid deceit, falsehood, and envy, these being vices unworthy of a Christian, that you be sober, faithful to your word, and above all charitable to the poor, and God will return to you again whatever you give for the love of Him. Particularly console the widows and orphans as much as will be in your power. Finally, avoid flatterers and take care that you never become one of them. It is a character equally odious and pernicious. The third thing which I recommend to you is again charity. That will never bring you to poverty ; and believe me whatever alms you give for the love of God will be profitable to both body and soul. Behold, this is all that I have to say to you. Neither your father nor I have a long time to live. God grant that before we die we may hear news of you which may bring honour upon ourselves and upon you. I commend you to the divine goodness.' "

Attend now to the modest answer of Bayard. " My Lady Mother, I thank you with all my heart for these good lessons which you have given to me ; and I hope, by the grace of Him to Whom you commend me, dearly to preserve them in memory and to give you satisfaction by my faithful practice."

### St. Louis ascends to heaven :

When St. Louis IX. of France was on his death-bed he commanded his family to be summoned and with his own hand he wrote out the following instructions which he committed to the prince who was to succeed him : " Fair son, the first thing which I teach thee and command thee to observe is this, that with all thy heart and above everything whatsoever thou love God, for without this no man can be saved. And guard thyself well against doing anything displeasing to Him, that is to say, sin. For thou oughtest rather to desire to suffer all manner· of torments than to sin mortally." — " If God shall visit thee with adversity receive it humbly and be grateful and consider that thou hast well deserved it, and that the whole will tend to thy good. If he shall give thee prosperity be thankful with humility and take care that thou be not corrupted by pride ; for we should not employ the gifts of God in service against Him. Let thy confessor be a wise and good man who can instruct thee in religion ; and take care that thy confessors, thy relations, and acquaintances, may be able boldly to reprove thy fault, whatever it may be. Attend the service of God and of our holy Mother the Church devoutly and with the service of heart and lips. Have a gentle and pitiful heart for the poor ; comfort and assist them as much as thou canst.  Maintain the good customs of thy kingdom and correct the bad. Be on thy guard against covetousness and against great taxing and subsidies unless the defence of thy kingdom shall require them.  If thy heart be sad or in trouble lay it open to thy confessor or to some good person who is discreet, and so thou wilt be enabled to endure thy misery.  Be sure that thou employ in thy company good and loyal men who are not covetous, whether ecclesiastics or others.  Fly from evil company ; and oblige thyself to hear the words of God and retain them in thy heart.  Continually desire prayer, instruction, and pardon.  Love thine honour.  Take heed that no man may be so hardy as to utter in thy presence any word which might tend to excite others to sin, that none should slander the absent or abuse those who are present.  Never permit anything to be uttered disrespectful towards God, the Holy Virgin, or the Saints.  Thank God often for His grace and for thy prosperity.  Exercise justice to all, to the poor as well as to the rich.  Let thy servants be loyal, liberal, and decisive in speech, that they may be feared and loved as their master.  If any dispute shall arise be exact in searching for the truth whether it be for or against thyself.  Love and honour churchmen and all ecclesiastics and take care that no person shall deprive them of their revenues, gifts, and alms, which thine ancestors have given to them.  I have been told that King Philip my grandfather answered a minister who said to him that the churchmen caused him to lose many rights and liberties and that it was a matter of wonder how he permitted it, by saying that he believed it to be so but that God had bestowed upon him so much grace and goodness that he had rather lose his wealth than have any dispute or contest with ministers of the Holy Church.  Honour and reverence thy father and mother and take care not to grieve them by disobedience to their commands.  Bestow the benefices which belong to thee upon good persons and those of pure manners.  Take heed how thou goest to war with a Christian man without deep reflection and unless the case is of necessity ; and on these occasions take care that neither the clergy nor those who have not injured thee may suffer. Take care also that no sin shall prevail in thy kingdom nor any blasphemy or heresy. And finally be mindful of me and my poor soul. And now I bestow all the blessings that a father can give to his child, praying to the whole Trinity of Paradise, the Father, the Son, and the Holy Ghost, that He may keep and defend thee from all evil, and especially from dying in mortal sin ; so that after this life ended we may meet again before God, to praise Him and return thanks forever in His kingdom of Paradise, Amen."

He then received the sacraments and caused himself to be placed on a bed of ashes. " The Cross was placed before his bed and before his eyes and he looked upon it full many times and towards it he turned his eyes. Furthermore, in that same sickness of his he frequently gave thanks to God his Creator and repeated very often the Pater Noster and the Miserere and the Credo." His brave and affectionate knights stood round him weeping. He did not speak for four days, remaining with his eyes raised towards heaven and his hands joined ; but from Sunday at time of none till Monday at time of tierce, says the King Thibaud of Navarre, who was an eye-witness, he uttered many prayers for his people, saying : " Be, O Lord, to Thy people a Sanctifier and a Guardian." About the hour of tierce he lost his speech, but looked at all the people about him with great kindness, and he smiled sometimes. Between tierce and midday he seemed to sleep with eyes closed. All remained kneeling in mournful silence. At length he opened his eyes, raised them towards heaven, and said : " I will come into Thy house : I will worship towards Thy holy temple." (20). "After that he spoke no more, and about the hour of none he passed away." "A pitiable thing it is," cries Joinville, " and worthy of weeping, the passing away of this holy Prince who has lived in such holiness and who has so well taken care of his kingdom and who had wrought so many fair deeds in the service of God." Velly has described the character of St. Louis in few words : " He possessed at once the sentiments of a true gentleman and the piety of the most humble Christian." The testimony of an infidel to the virtues of this great King is striking. To him Louis IX. appeared a prince destined to reform Europe, if that had been possible, to render France victorious, and to be in all things a model for men. His

55

piety, which was that of an anchorite, deprived him of no virtue belonging to a king. A wise economy interfered not with his liberality. He knew how to reconcile a profound political sagacity with an exact justice ; and perhaps he is the only sovereign who merits this praise. Prudent and firm he was in counsel, intrepid in battle without rashness, pitiful as if he had always been unhappy. " It is not given to man to carry virtue to a greater length." Attacked by the plague before Tunis, he caused himself to be stretched upon ashes, and expired in his 55th year, with the piety of a monk and the courage of a great man. How deplorable to reflect that we can neither admire nor reverence the master who has bequeathed this portrait to prosperity !

**Bayard's death :**
It is impossible to read without being moved the simple account which has been handed down to us of the death, the prayer, and the last words of the incomparable Bayard, a name which no hero will ever pronounce without reverence and love. When he received the fatal wound his first cry was : " Jesus ; ah, my God, I am dead !" Then he kissed the handle of his sword for want of a cross. He changed colour, and his men, seeing him stagger, ran, and were about to carry him out of the press of battle. His friend D'Alègre endeavoured to persuade him but he would not permit it. " It is all over with me," he said, " I am a dead man : I should be sorry in my last moments, and for the first time in my life, to turn my back to the enemy." He had still the strength to order a charge when he saw that the Spaniards were beginning to advance. Then he caused himself to be placed by some Swiss at the foot of a tree, " so that," said he, "I may have my face to the enemy." These were his words. His steward, who was a gentleman of Dauphiné named Jaques Jeoffré de Milieu, burst into tears by his side as did also the other attendants while Bayard endeavoured to console them. " It is the will of God," said he, " to draw me to Himself. He has preserved me long enough in this world and He has bestowed upon me more mercy and grace than I have ever deserved." Then, in the absence of a priest who could hear his confession sacramentally, according to the

custom of the time he made his confession to his gentleman, whom he commanded to take care that he was not moved, since the least motion occasioned insupportable pain. The Seigneur D'Alègre Mayor of Paris asked what were his last wishes and he received them. Then immediately Jean Diesbac a Swiss captain proposed to remove him for fear that he should fall into the hands of the enemy ; but he said to him as well as to all the officers who stood around : " Leave me to think of my conscience for the few moments I have to live. I beseech you to retire lest you should be made prisoners and that should be an addition to my pain. It is all over with me ; you can be of no assistance to me in anything. All that I beg of you to do for me, Seigneur D'Alègre, is to assure the King that I die his servant and only regretting that I cannot serve him any more. Present my respects to my lords the Princes of France and to all the gentlemen and captains. Farewell my good friends ; I recommend to you my poor soul." Upon this they took their last leave of him and retired. At the same moment the Marquis of Pescara came up to him and with tears in his eyes exlaimed : " Would to God, Seigneur Bayard, that I had shed my blood, as much as I could lose without dying, to have you now my prisoner in good health. You should know how much I have always esteemed your person, your courage, and all the virtues which you possess and for which I have never known your equal." He then caused his own tent to be carried and spread round the dying man, and he assisted him to place himself upon a bed. He placed a guard to take care that no one should plunder or disturb him, and he himself went for a priest, to whom Bayard confessed in full possession of his faculties and with an edifying piety. The Spanish army from the highest to the lowest hastened to admire the expiring hero. The Constable of Bourbon came with the others and said : "Ah Captain Bayard how saddened and troubled I am to see you in this state ! I have always loved and honoured you for the great prowess and wisdom which you possess. Ah what great pity I have for you !" Bayard summoned up his failing strength and with a firm voice made him that answer for ever memorable : " Monseigneur, I thank you. There is nothing to pity in me, who die as an honourable man, serving my King. There is need to pity you, who carry arms against your Prince, your country, and your oath." The Constable remained a short time with him and gave him his reasons for having left the kingdom ; but Bayard exhorted him to seek the King's pardon and favour. Then he was left alone. And now he thought only of death. He devoutly recited the psalm *Miserere mei Deus* ; after which he prayed in the following words with a loud voice : "O my God, Who hast promised an asylum in Thy pity for the greatest sinners who return to Thee sincerely and with all their heart, in Thee do I place my trust, and in Thy promises all my hope. Thou art my God, my Creator, my Redeemer. I confess that against Thee I have mortally offended and that a thousand years of fasting upon bread and water in the desert could never efface my sins. But, my God, Thou knowest that I had resolved to repent if Thou hadst prolonged my life. I know all my weakness and that by myself I never should have been able to merit an entrance into Paradise, and that no creature can obtain it save through Thine infinite mercy. O my God, my Father, forget my sins, listen only to Thy clemency. Let Thy justice be appeased by the merits of the blood of Jesus Christ "— death cut short the sentence. " His first cry," says the amiable M. de Berville, who has written his life, " when he felt himself mortally wounded, was the Name of Jesus." And it was pronouncing this adorable Name that the hero yielded up his soul to its Creator on the 30th April 1524 in the 48th year of his age.

**Last victories :**

With the name of Charlemagne is connected all the wonder of history, all the images of fiction, and every kind of renown. " His political wisdom," says Mably, " should supply lessons to kings of the most enlightened age." " The glory of succeeding times," says Marchangy, " has not deprived this monarch of our admiration. Neither our heroic misfortunes on the banks of the Jordan, nor the carousals and tournaments of Chivalry, neither the victories of Bovines and Marignan, of Fribourg and Marseilles, nor all the palms of Philip and Louis, all the laurels of Du Guesclin and Bayard, can make the children of the muses forget what they owe to Charlemagne.

Let us view him on his death-bed. The heavens seemed to participate in the great event of his departure. He saw his death approach with the same intrepidity which he would have shown in battle. He was occupied in correcting a copy of the Holy Scriptures when the fever of death came on. His last effort, on the eighth day of his illness, was to lift up his feeble right hand and make the sign of the Cross on his forehead and breast. After this he composed his limbs and expired with these words: '*In manus tuas commendo spiritum meum: redemisti me, Domine, Deus veritatis.*'" (21). He died on the 28th of January 814 in the 72nd year of his age.

The character of his son Louis is thus described: "He was slow to anger, quick to compassion. Every day early he would go to pray in the church, where he remained with bent knees, touching the pavement with his forehead, humbly praying, and sometimes with tears. He was adorned with innocent manners. He never wore golden robes unless on the great feasts, as was the custom with his fathers. Daily before meat he gave large alms." His times were troublesome, but he was a virtuous and a very learned king.

Turn we now to witness the last moments of the great Orlando, wounded to death at Ronceval, as related by Archbishop Turpin. The following was his prayer: "O Lord Jesus, to Thee do I commit my soul in this trying hour. Thou Who didst suffer on the Cross for those who deserved not Thy favour deliver my soul, I beseech Thee, from eternal death. I confess myself a most grievous sinner, but Thou mercifully dost forgive our sins. Thou pitiest everyone and hatest nothing which Thou hast made, covering the sins of the repentant in whatsoever day they turn unto Thee with true contrition. O Thou Who didst spare Thy enemies, and the woman taken in adultery, Who didst pardon Mary Magdalen, and look with compassion on the weeping Peter, Who didst likewise open the gates of Paradise to the Thief that confessed to Thee upon the cross, have mercy upon me and receive my soul into Thy everlasting rest." Then, stretching out his hands towards heaven, he prayed for the souls of those who perished in the battle ; and immediately after this prayer his soul winged its flight to God.

## Maxims of Christian Chivalry

In witnessing scenes of this melancholy grandeur the admiration and astonishment of the historical student will be continually excited. " It is an instructive example for men in all conditions of life to witness the death of a great man who unites noble sentiments with Christian humility." This is the observation of the French historian Anquetil when he prepares to relate the tragical death of the gallant Montmorenci, who was abandoned by the Duke of Orleans to the resentment of his brother Louis XIII. or rather, perhaps, of Richelieu. Permission, it seems, had been granted to him to have his hands at liberty on going to execution, but he refused to avail himself of this indulgence. " A great sinner like me," he said, " cannot die with ignominy enough." Of his own accord he took off his superb dress in which he was at liberty to have appeared. " Shall I then care," he said, " being so criminal as I am, to go to death with vanity, while my innocent Saviour dies all naked on the Cross ?" Every action of his last moments was marked with the seal of Christianity. He was so full of hope that he seemed rather to desire than to fear death. There did not escape from him either complaint or murmur. He stepped with firmness upon the scaffold, placed his head upon the block, and cried to the executioner: " Strike boldly " ! and he received the blow in commending his soul to God. How affecting were the words of Don Juan Padilla to Don Juan Bravo when they were being led to execution for their revolt in the reign of Charles V. and when they were publicly denounced as traitors. Bravo gave vent to his indignation, but Padilla reproved him, saying : " Yesterday was the time to display the courage of a knight ; to-day it is the time to die with the meekness of a Christian !"

### Facing death :

Of this more than regal dignity one of the most illustrious human examples that the world has ever beheld was presented by Louis IX. in prison. This meek and humble saint was more than conqueror over his enemies, who declared that " this was the fiercest Christian whom they had ever known." In vain did they threaten him with the most dreadful torture, that which they called putting him in bernicles, by means of which invention every bone of the body was gradually broken. The King answered with modesty : " I am a prisoner of the Sultan ; he can do with me as he wills." What an astonishing scene of horror and grandeur was that when the Saracen rebel, after murdering the Sultan, rushed into the prison in which the King was, with his hands dropping blood, and cried out with a ferocious voice : " What will you give me for having made away with an enemy who would have put you to death if he had lived ?" Louis, more struck with horror at the crime than with fear for his own safety, remained motionless and disdained to answer. Then the ruffian drawing his sword presented the point at him, saying with an accent of fury : " Choose either to die by this hand or else to give me this very moment the order of knighthood." " Make thyself a Christian," answered the intrepid monarch, " and I will make thee a knight." The Musulman rushed out of the prison.

**Death with joy :**

St. Elzear was of the ancient and illustrious family of Sabran in Provence. His father Hermengaud de Sabran was created Count of Arian in the kingdom of Naples. His mother was Lauduna of Alba of a family no less distinguished for its nobility. The Count was born in 1295 at his father's castle of Ansois in the diocese of Apt. He was effianced in his childhood to Delphina of Glandeves, daughter of the Lord of Pui-Michel. The following are among the regulations which were established in his family at the castle where he and his lady resided : " Everyone in my house shall daily hear Mass. If God be well served nothing will be wanting. Let no one swear or curse or blaspheme, under pain of being severely chastised and afterwards shamefully dismissed from my service. Can I hope that God will pour forth His heavenly blessings on my house if it is filled with such miscreants, who devote themselves to the devil ? I will have no playing at dice or any games of hazard. There are a thousand innocent diversions, though time passes away soon enough without being idly thrown away. Yet I desire not my castle to be a cloister nor my people hermits. Let them be merry, and sometimes let them divert themselves, but never at the expense of conscience or with danger of offending God. I will not have my coffers filled by emptying those of others, or by squeezing the blood out of the veins, and the marrow out of the bones of the poor. Such bloodsucking, wicked servants, to enrich their masters, damn both their masters and themselves. Do you imagine that a master who gives five shillings in alms wipes away the theft of his servants who have torn out the entrails of the poor, whose cries for vengeance mount to heaven?" St. Elzear would feign to be hunting the stag while he was in quest of poor people; he would mount his horse with his falconers, with his hawk on his wrist, being attended by his servants with the dogs, and presently he would slip aside into the forest and seek some miserable hut to assist the poor. Though a great saint he was not the less a chivalrous prince. He bore away the prize before the court of Naples; he conquered at many tournaments; he was a valiant commander and gained military victories in Italy. When he was dying and when the priest who was assisting him came to the words: "Through Thy Cross and Passion deliver him O Lord." (22), he interrupted him and said aloud: " This is my hope, in this hope I wish to die." Of such men St. Augustine says : " He does not die with patience, but he lives with patience and dies with joy." (23).

### A flower of Christian Chivalry :

In the old life of St. Gerald, Count of Aurillac, it is said : "We are told that his parents held to modesty and religion as if these gifts came to them by inheritance. 'The generation of the righteous shall be blessed.'"(24). We often see little children given to anger and envy and vengeance, "but in the boy Gerald we see a certain sweetness of character together with modesty." After being instructed in the chant and in grammar, when he became a youth he grew expert at arms and would vault upon his horse with ease. Though engaged in military exercises still he studied hard, according to the advice given in holy Scripture: "Wisdom is better than strength."(25). He soon became acquainted with the whole volume of the Holy Scriptures. His parents dying he succeeded to his territories, but no pride followed; he only lamented that he had to be occupied too often in worldly affairs. He now considered all his vassals

as his pupils and wards.   In all his wars, though valiant to the
utmost, he never wounded anyone, nor was himself wounded,
and, by God's grace, his sword was never dyed in human blood.
Other men are valiant and generous, but they are so for the
world's sake.   " But the work of Gerald is luminous because
it is the fruit of simplicity of heart."

The ancient deceiver of the ways of youth laid his snares for
Gerald ; but he had learned to fly by prayer to the bosom of
God's fatherly care and to counteract those snares by the grace
of Christ.   He was remarkable for abstemiousness at table and
for devotion at the divine offices which he used to attend before
daybreak.   He used himself to recite the whole Psalter every
day.   He was beautiful in person, of perfect innocence in
morals, the elegance of his body adorning the sweetness of his
mind.   No harsh or unseemly word ever escaped him.   He was
not only himself sober but he took care that all his people and
guests should be so ; so that none rose up from his table either
dizzy or yet sad.   He never broke his fast till tierce.   Seats
and tables for the poor were placed before him that he might
see they were well fed.   Nor was the number fixed, but all
comers were welcome ; and this he did believing that in
relieving them he relieved Christ.   So he provided them with
meat and clothes and shoes.   At meal time, once a day, he
observed the greatest sanctity and reverence.   Three days in
the week he abstained from meat.   There was always free
access to him, and his benevolence was known far and wide.
When he heard of dissensions among the common people
he would have Mass celebrated by way of suffrage for them.
The only shadow of injustice to be laid to his charge was his
seeming to lean always to the side of the poor and the weak.
He was a simple and a firm and a just man, and he would
execute justice, hoping too, in regard to the criminals, " that
by temporal punishment they might atone for the crime
which could not be allowed to remain unpunished."   " In
every work of piety he so ordered himself that his piety could
not be too much observed."   He was often reproached for
suffering himself to be injured by persons of low condition
without showing proper spirit and anger.   His peasants and
clergy loved him as a father.   They would bring him presents
of wax which he would receive as if they were vast presents.

Yet he would not burn this wax for his own use but had it employed at the altar. He often used larchwood torches, and would always have a light burning in his chamber that he might read at intervals about the love of Christ. Deservedly he was loved by all, for he loved all ; and he was called Gerald the Good. According to the Apostle's precept : He lived " soberly, and justly, and godly." (26). The holy Bishop Gaubert was most familiar with him and dear to him. With this prelate he often conversed, and said how he wished to go to Rome, and how he desired to enter a Religious order. But the bishop persuaded him to remain in the world that he might continue to defend and comfort the poor peasants. So he sacrificed himself for the love of his neighbour. But secretly he took the tonsure, and made a journey to Rome, and on his return built a great monastery and church. He lamented bitterly the want of piety and innocence in men ; yet he was unwilling to be always reproaching them. So he prayed that Almighty God would give them peace, and he had Mass celebrated for this intention, continually repeating with Ezechias : " Only let peace and truth be in my days " (27) ; and again : "Oh how truly it may be said : ' There is now no saint.' " (28). Good monks are like angels, he would say ; but if to secular desires they fall then they are like the apostate angels. It appeared from all his words and deeds that he had no love for the world and that he panted after heaven. At supper he had lessons read aloud. Whenever he commenced any action he repeated some holy verse, doing all things according to the apostolic precept. Sometimes when he was with few persons, as if he were lost in meditation, some tears would be seen to fall from him, so that it was clear his mind was elsewhere fixed and had no present consolation. " And as of old the dove of Noe, when it found no resting place outside the Ark, returned to the Ark and to Noe himself, so that man, in the midst of the waves of this world, betook himself to the secret chamber of his own heart and there found his rest and delight in Christ." At night he used to remain alone after the office and enjoy internal peace. He used to go to Rome every second year, and it was a happy journey for all the poor of the countries through which he passed. When would Count Gerald come ? was the usual question of the mountaineers who inhabited the passages of the great Mount St. Bernard. Many wonders and miracles are said to have been wrought through his means. " Yet those who are captivated by a pious love of him and who venerate him with a prudent affection are better pleased by the works of justice which he practised than by those wonders. The greatest of his miracles was his not trusting in riches." And now his outward man began to fail, while the inward was renewed day by day. He became blind and continued so for seven years, that the man of God might be proved in this world of sorrow. And therefore he gave thanks to God that he was worthy to suffer as a son. And so he gave himself up to constant prayer. Two years before he died he built a great church and procured many relics of saints. And now his sickness came on to death, and so he cried : " Subvenite Sancti Dei." (29). He sent for Amblard, a holy bishop, to fortify him for his passage, and he gave orders respecting his funeral. And now the report of his state drew crowds of clergy, monks, nobles, poor people, weeping and praying. O good Gerald, what a loss to the world when you depart ! The father of the poor, the defender of widows, the comforter of the miserable ! And so they lamented at his death. O truly happy death ! O happy man who, raised on high in secular power, injured no one, oppressed no one ! He heard Mass to the last and would be carried into his oratory. He expired sweetly on a Friday, 13th October, 909, at Complin time, with the words : " Subvenite Sancti Dei."

### Knightly counsels :

Let us take an instance from an old romance. When King Perceforest was about to knight his son Berthis and his nephew he thus addressed them : " He who wishes to enter an order, whether it be into religion or marriage or Chivalry, or into whatever state it may be, first he ought to purify and cleanse his conscience from all vices and to fill and adorn it with all the virtues and to have an ardent desire to persevere till the end for the love of the Sovereign God. My children wash your hearts and your consciences from all stains by true repentance and by prayer for mercy and make your petitions to the Sovereign God." " When the King had said this the

E

youths and the King too knelt in front of an altar which was before them and prayed for a long space until the King knew that through the weakness of nature devotion could no longer last." Then rising up he taught them that there was but one God. " My children if you fear God all things of the world will fear you, and if you fear not God you will fear all the things that you shall see." Then he gives them counsel to all virtue. " Fair sons we ought to live for two things, that is to say our honour and our salvation. Be united with your equals, be humble towards your lord, and to all those who are under you be a faithful administrator of justice. And love your Creator above all. By my faith it is a fair thing for a prince to have knowledge, and a foul thing, as well as dangerous for his country, for him to be ignorant. He that knows well his Creator cannot have a bad ending. He who cannot conquer himself has no right to conquer anyone else. Fair sons, everything passes away but one thing : to love God."

**Orate fratres :**
The Moors of Granada had such confidence in the honour of Pedro King of Aragon that their King refused to take any precaution when the former was fitting out a great armament, since he had a treaty of five years with him ; and he said : " The house of Aragon is the house of God, of faith, and of honour." When the King of Aragon came to die,—it was on the festival of St. Martin,—having made his devout confession and received the other sacraments, having caused his will to be read aloud and ordered his body to be buried in the monastery of the Holy Cross, after taking leave of the queen and the infantas and giving them his blessing, he caused a cross to be brought to him. He took it in his hands and wept devoutly and made a good prayer. Lifting up his eyes towards heaven he crossed himself three times, embraced the cross, and then said : " O Lord, our Father, true God Jesus Christ, into Thy hands I commend my spirit. Deign by Thy holy Passion, which Thou hast suffered, to receive my soul into Paradise with the blessed St. Martin, whose festival Christians celebrate on this day." And then, with eyes still raised towards heaven, he departed.

**Practices of devotion :**

The simplicity and zeal with which the ordinary exercises of devotion were observed deserve attention. Ste. Palaye informs us, upon the authority of the doctrinal manuscripts of St. Germain, that the knights of old never allowed themselves to be absent from the morning service of the Church as soon as they were risen ; and we meet with continual instances of this practice, both in private annals and in the public conduct of the camp, in Froissart, Joinville's history of St. Louis, the Ancient Chronicles, the lives of Bayard, Du Guesclin, Francis I, and even Henry IV. of France. Every one knows the famous saying of this last named monarch when he and his army fell upon their knees before the battle of Coutras : " We cannot humble ourselves too much before God nor be too bold towards men." What a description of Charlemagne is given by Eginhart ! " He observed with the utmost piety and veneration the Christian religion with which he had been imbued from childhood. He frequented the church early and late, even at the night office whenever his health permitted him. Even his banquet-hall had a religious solemnity about it. Twelve varlets stood round holding lighted tapers, while a clerk read aloud a chapter from St. Augustine's *De Civitate Dei.*"

**Hardy and courageous :**

Froissart relates how the Earl of Pembroke, when besieged in the house of the Templars near Poitiers, despatched a squire upon his best horse to Sir John Chandos. The squire " departed at the hour of mydnight, and al the night he rode out of his way, and when it was mornyng and fayre day, then he knew his way, and so rode towards Poitiers, and by that tyme his horse was weary : howbeit he came thyder by nyne of the clocke, and ther alyghted before Sir John Chandos' lodgyng, and entred and founde him at Masse, and so came and kneeled down before him, and dyde his message as he was commanded." This was the famous Sir John Chandos whom Du Guesclin called : "the moost renowmed knight of the worlde," and Froissart : " a right hardy and courageous knight who was slain in battle and lamented by his friends and his foes."

**What the world says of prayer :**

They accused St. Louis of devoting too much time to his prayers. " Men are strange," he answered with sweetness ; " they make it a crime in me that I am assiduous at prayer, and they would not say a word if I were to employ the hours which I give to prayer in games of hazard or in hunting wild beasts or hawking for birds."

**Praying regularly :**

But let us return to the Chevalier Bayard. " He loved and feared God," says the President d'Expilly in the conclusion of his eulogy. " He had always recourse to Him in difficulty, praying regularly both morning and evening ; for which purpose he would be always alone."

**No rhetoric :**

Even St. John Chrysostom shunned the style of orators, and, though he was naturally as eloquent as Demosthenes, yet he adopted no exordium, no division, and appears not even to have formed a plan for his discourse.

**Shelter in the cloister :**

We shall meet with many instances in history and romance where knights, kings, and emperors, have sought in the cloister a refuge from the misery of the world. When Sir Launcelot recovered from his swoon caused by the wound in his side he cried out : " O Lauayne help me that I were on my horse, for here is fast by within this two mile a gentle knight that some time was a full noble knight and a great lord of possessions. And for great goodness he hath taken him to wilful poverty and forsaken many lands, and his name is Sire Baudewyn of Bretayne, and he is a full noble surgeon and a good leech." And the hermit says of himself : " For some time I was one of the fellowship of the Round Table ; but I thank God, now I am otherwise disposed." " And then anon the hermit staunched his blood and made him to drink good wine ; so that Sir Launcelot was well refreshed and knew himself. For in these days it was not the guise of hermits as is nowadays. For there were none hermits in those days but that they had been men of worship and of prowess. And

68

those hermits held great household and refreshed people that were in distress." Sir Launcelot himself ends his life in a hermit's habit. After taking leave of the Queen "he rode all that day and all that night in a forest weeping. And at the last he was ware of a hermitage and a chapel that stood between the cliffs, and then he heard a little bell ring to Mass, and thither he rode and alighted and tied his horse to the gate and heard Mass. And he that sang the Mass was the Bishop of Canterbury. Both the Bishop and Sir Bedwere knew Sir Launcelot, and they spoke together after Mass. But when Sir Bedwere had told him his tale Sir Launcelot's heart almost broke for sorrow. And Sir Launcelot threw abroad his armour and said : 'Alas, who may trust this world !' And then he knelt down on his knees and prayed the Bishop for to shrive and assoil him. And then he besought the Bishop that he might be his brother. Then the Bishop said : 'I will gladly.' And then he put a habit upon Sir Launcelot, and then he served God day and night with prayers and fastings." In like manner Sir Bors comes to the chapel and follows his example. So does Sir Galyhud, Sir Galyhodyn, Sir Bleoberys, Sir Villyars, Sir Clarrus, and Sir Gahalantyne. "And when they saw that Sir Launcelot had taken him to such perfection they had no list to depart but took such a habit as he had. Thus they endured in great penance six years, and then Sir Launcelot took the habit of priesthood, and after a twelvemonth he sang Mass."

### The voice of nature :
"Oh what a goodly thing it is," cries Caussin, "to talk face to face with those great forests which are born with the world, to discourse with the murmur of waters and the warbling of birds in the sweetness of solitude." "Believe me upon my own experience," said St. Bernard to those whom he invited into his Order, "thou wilt find something more in the woods than in books ; the trees and rocks will teach thee what thou canst not hear from masters." (30).

### Fruits of solitude :
But what fiction can excite greater interest than is produced by the real history of Fr. Thomas of Jesus of the Order of the

## Maxims of Christian Chivalry

Hermits of St. Augustine, whose work on the *Sufferings of Christ*, written in Portuguese and translated into many languages, has lent wings to many a soul now in the bliss of Paradise ? This holy religious was son of Ferdinand Alvarez de Andrada of one of the chief families in Portugal. In 1578 King Dom Sebastian made him quit his solitude and accompany him on the unfortunate expedition into Africa. He was made prisoner on the day when the King was slain. Hence it was in a dungeon, in chains, without clothes, and with but little food, that he wrote this admirable book, writing only in the middle of the day by the help of a faint light which he received through an air-hole. On being sold to a merchant he made it his care to instruct the poor Christian slaves and to make many converts. He refused the offer of money which was collected in Portugal and sent for his ransom ; and he died on Easter Monday, pronouncing the name of Jesus, after having strengthened in the faith some miserable slaves who had been inclined to turn Mahommedans through despair of otherwise obtaining freedom. The great Cardinal Ximenes in the year of his entering the Order of St. Francis built with his own hands a hut in a thick unfrequented wood of chestnut trees and frequently spent in it many successive days in prayer and study. This he always described as the happiest part of his life. In a late period of his career he declared that he would willingly exchange all his dignities for his hut in the chestnut wood.

**Quis separabit :**
The holy abbot Deicolus was asked how he was able to maintain such a continual cheerfulness. " Because no one can take Christ away from me," was his answer.

**Tears of joy :**
Surius relates that Pope Innocent II., having gone to visit the monastery of Clairvaux all the monks came out to meet him with St. Bernard, and that the Pope and all the Cardinals were so affected at the sight of that holy congregation that they wept for joy and reverence.

**Royal charity :**

"In short, it would be impossible to relate the number and greatness of the acts of charity which were performed by the King St. Louis," says Joinville. "When some persons complained of this expense he answered that he loved better to go to great expense in giving alms than to spend the money on good cheer and vanities." And the historian adds that, for all his alms, their was nothing deficient in the expenditure of his house or unworthy of a great prince. Wherever he travelled within his kingdom he was in the habit of visiting the poor churches and hospitals. He would inquire for poor gentlemen and widows, and for young ladies who were in distress, that he might enable them to marry. Wherever there was suffering and distress, there he bestowed his money and his interest. The commissioners whom he sent into the provinces to make restitution were directed to draw up a list of the poor labourers of each parish who were disabled, and these were provided for by the King. His will contained a vast number of donations to monasteries and hospitals, to poor young women for their dowry, to the poor in general who wanted clothing, to scholars who had not the means of defraying the expense of their education, to widows and orphans, and lastly to clerics until they should procure a benefice. It is related of King Robert, son of Hugh Capet, that he fed three hundred poor persons every day. Upon Maundy Thursday he served them on his knees and washed their feet ; and thence the custom prevailed in France, as in Germany, for the King to perform this pious ceremony every year.

**No waiting tears :**

Upon a height within the castle of the Counts of Champagne in Troyes was a tower whence the whole city was visible. Here Thibault of fair descent used to receive two monks every day who were charged to search out the poor and miserable of the city and bring their report to him. When they had found no object for charity he used to show them the vast city below and say : "Are there indeed no tears to wipe away here ? Blessed be God Who protects my people." Then he used to sing a Latin hymn with the monks.

## Maxims of Christian Chivalry

**Knightly vigils :**

Nothing can mark in stronger colours the tone of deep religious feeling which was to be the foundation and essence of Chivalry than the custom of keeping vigils in a church previous to being admitted to the order of knighthood, and afterwards upon different occasions when the circumstances or inclinations of individuals might require it. "It was the custom of the English," says Ingulphus, "that he who was to be consecrated a knight, on the eve of his consecration should confess all his sins with contrition to a Bishop or abbot or monk or priest, and being absolved should devote himself to prayer and piety and affliction, and should spend the night in a church. The next morning at Mass he should offer his sword on the altar, and after the gospel the priest should place the blessed sword on the neck of the warrior, who, having communicated in the sacred mysteries of Christ at the same Mass, then became a legitimate knight." The same ceremonies were observed in all Christian states, with the exception of Normandy where the Danish and more military form prevailed. The reader will find, upon reference to Ste. Palaye or Büsching, that nights passed in prayer and fasting in a church, a confession of sins, the Blessed Sacrament received with devotion, attention to the sermon in which the priest explained the articles of faith and Christian morality, were generally the preliminary steps for obtaining the honour of knighthood. "The night before any one was to assume the spurs," says an old writer, "it behoved him to be armed cap-a-pee and so armed to repair unto the church and to stand there on his feet or kneel in prayer all the live-long night." The *Siete Partidas*, quoted by the author of *Roderick*, gives very particular directions. "The squire shall be taken to the church where he is to labour in watching and beseeching mercy of God that He will forgive him his sins and guide him so that he may demean himself well in that order which he is about to receive ; to the end that he may defend the divine law and do all other things according as it behoveth him, and that God would be his defender and keeper in all danger and in all difficulties. And he ought to bear in mind how God is powerful above all things and can show His power in them when he listeth and especially in affairs of arms. For in His hand are life and death to give and to take away, and He can make the weak strong and the strong weak. And when he is making this prayer he must be with his knees bent, and all the rest of the time on foot, as long as he can bear it. For the vigil of knights was not ordained to be a sport, nor for anything else except that they, and those who accompanied them, should pray to God to protect them and direct them in the right way and support them as men who are entering upon the way of death."

### The Christian woman :
The Christian religion secured the purity and the elevation of the female heart ; and it was the consequent influence of women, that empire which they obtained by the power of virtue, meekness, and innocence, over the wild affections of our brave ancestors, which contributed greatly to effect a marvellous revolution in the moral history of the world.

### Mary a mirror :
" Therefore," says St. Ambrose, " let the virginity and life of Mary be as if painted in a picture before you, from which, as from a mirror, let the image of chastity and the pattern of virtue be reflected . . . In her eyes there is nothing haughty, in her words nothing insolent, in her actions nothing opposed to modesty." (31).

### The arch's other side :
That this affection extended to all women and that women were honoured and loved also in an especial manner from this religious consideration appears upon sufficient evidence. Among the " poets in praise of women " who flourished in Germany under the Suabian emperors, Henry of Mainz, celebrated under the name of Doctor Frauenlob, composed a poem in praise of women which he dedicated to the Emperor Henry VII. In this he says : " THE MOTIVES WHICH OBLIGE CHRISTIANS TO LOVE THE BLESSED VIRGIN SHOULD BIND THEM ALSO TO HONOUR AND LOVE ALL WOMEN," (32).

### The devout sex :
The conduct and sentiments which women adopted from

the first in respect to the Christian religion contributed to confirm men in this judgment and to secure for themselves the love and veneration of all who worshipped Christ. William of Paris points out the peculiar devotion with which women followed our Blessed Saviour. From His Birth to His Death and Resurrection they were ever pressing forward to adore and serve Him. After His Crucifixion, on the morning of the third day, when it was yet dark, the holy women were at the Sepulchre.

### Reverence for true womanhood :

" All virtue lies in woman," says a knight, " and the health of the world. No one can find a limit to the praise of women. He who can tell where the sunshine ends may proclaim also the end of their praise. Women are pure and good and fair ; they impart worthiness and make men worthy. Nothing is so like the angels as their beautiful form, and even the mind of an angel dwells in woman."

### A faithful wife :

When Guy Earl of Warwick returns to England in the habit of a pilgrim, after an absence of seven years in the holy land, coming to his castle he beholds the Countess sitting at the gate and distributing alms to a crowd of poor people, ordering them all to pray for the safe return of her lord from Palestine.

### St. Elizabeth of Hungary :

The castle of Marburg, the residence of the Landgrave of Hesse, was built on a steep rock which the infirm and weak were not able to climb. The Margravine Elizabeth (33) therefore built a hospital at the foot of the rock where they could be received and cared for and where she often fed them with her own hands. She fed nine hundred persons daily at her gate, not encouraging idleness, but giving employment to all who were able to work.

### Holy queens :

Massillon was so profoundly impressed with a sense of the holiness which had distinguished the early Queens of France that in praying for the young King he could imagine

74

no words more suitable to express his desire than these :
" God of my fathers ! save the son of Adelaide, of Blanche,
and of Clotilde."

## God's graces first :

An old writer says of the Blessed Delphine Countess de
Sabran : " To be in the good graces of Madame it was necessary to be in the good graces of God."

## When the earth was nearer heaven :

In the sixth century it was common for nuns, without going
into a monastic community, to live in their family house,
where they were secluded, unless on the festivals, when they
went to the churches.   St. Radegonde founded at Poitiers the
convent of the Holy Cross which was the first abbey of women
that was seen in France.

## The mother of freedom :

Montesquieu concluded that the ancient religion agreed
better with a monarchy and that the protestant religion
was more adapted to a republic ; but M. de Haller in the
sixth volume of his work on the Restoration of Political
Science has shown the fallacy of this sophistical decision.
" The principle of the moderns," he argues, " is absolutely
destructive of a republic ; and if fully developed—for it is often
counteracted by the ancient spirit—it would prove so in every
instance.   The spirit of the moderns is manifestly not a spirit
of union, but much rather of dividing asunder and of
separation.   By virtue of this spirit every individual knows
all things, understands all things, even what he does not
know, and places no faith in the authority of older or
wiser men.   With such a disposition no union is possible,
or it could be established only by unjust compulsion.
It can have neither strength nor continuance ; and a republic
in which every man may create and explain separate
constitutions, laws, and usages, after his own judgment,
could no more stand than a church in which every member
would be authorized to define according to his own private
views the faith, the morals, and the ceremonial of worship.
On the other hand, the relationship of a republic or civil

community, which binds men together through common principles and wants, requires, much more than a monarchy, a constant sacrifice of the individual, a resignation to the community, a reverence for antiquity and custom and ancestral tradition. Nowhere would the private interpretation and the selfish will be more frequently humbled, nowhere must it be more submissive to the common faith, and the common will. And it cannot be denied that inasmuch as the ancient religion is founded on that same principle more than the modern religion is, so the ancient religion is peculiarly adapted to develop and inspire that virtue of submission. Experience also shows that the ancient religion unites itself with all common relations and particularly with a republic. The republic of Venice lasted for one thousand four hundred years, and other Italian states did not ascribe the loss of their freedom to their religion. The Swiss republics were founded and strengthened when all hearts were still united through the old and general faith. No one has thought of writing their history since the divisions of the Church, as if from a melancholy conviction that they had nothing more in them that was great and renowned and worthy to be handed down to posterity. In the free democratic mountain-valleys of Switzerland was internal peace preserved almost without interruption, and only by means of the Catholic religion, under many various and complicated relations. It is still the only rein, the only garrison, and it preserves real freedom, while it is a fact that the republics of Geneva and Holland and many others were so often torn by internal divisions."

### Comfortable vulgarity :

It is well known that a distinguishing characteristic of everything belonging to the early and middle ages of Christianity is the picturesque. Those who now struggle to cultivate the fine arts are obliged to have recourse to the despised and almost forgotten houses, towns, and dresses, of those periods. As soon as men renounced the philosophy of the Church it was inevitable that their taste, that the form of objects under their control, should change with their religion. For architects had no longer to provide for the love of solitude, of meditation between sombre pillars, of modesty in apartments with the lancet-casement. They were not to study duration and solidity in an age when men were taught to regard the present as their only concern. When nothing but exact knowledge was sought after the undefined sombre arches were to be removed to make way for lines which would proclaim their brevity, and for a blaze of light which might correspond with the mind of those who rejected every proposition that led beyond the reach of the senses and who wished to believe that there was nothing in the world but what they saw and touched. When money was to be the recognized object of even poetic ambition no marvel that merchants required a quicker communication by more artificial roads, that citizens were eager to pull down gates and crosses and whatever might impede the operations of commerce. As men no longer made vows of poverty, or rather, as poverty became a disgrace, every object was to put on that neat, glaring, varnished, surface of wealth, which is so intractable to the pencil. The revival of the epicurean philosophy, which Cicero thought so unfavourable to eloquence, must quickly appear in the furniture, in the whole plan and form of life. The revival of the cynic philosophy must appear in the show of outward hideousness in dress, which purposely sets grace and gentleness at defiance, and in the very gait and countenance of men. This was all natural and unavoidable.

### Blessed are the poor :

" For theirs is the kingdom of heaven." (34). " Poverty has in some sense a broad wing by means of which the flight to the kingdom of heaven is quickly accomplished." This is the remark of St. Bernard upon those words of Holy Scripture. " For in the case of other virtues," he says, " which are here subsequently mentioned the reward is indicated by a promise for the time to come ; but to poverty it is rather given than promised. Hence the reward is here announced as belonging to the present time : ' For theirs is the kingdom of heaven,' whereas in regard the other virtues the words are : ' They shall possess, they shall be comforted,' and such like." (35).

77

# Maxims of Christian Chivalry

**Novelty dangerous :**

What but deep meditation induced Montaigne, in an age given to introducing new religions, to say : " I am disgusted with novelty, whatever face it wears, and I have reasons for being so. The best title that can be given to novelty is : very dangerous."

**Religion of motives :**

In the very beginning of this research we said that the religion of Chivalry was a religion of motives. " All this counts for nothing without faith," said one of the accusers of Jacques Molay, when the latter had concluded an eloquent statement of the heroic virtues of the Order of the Temple. The answer of the Grand Master showed a deeper wisdom. " Without faith," he answered, " nothing of all this could be borne." So Chivalry was taught by religion that actions were fully worthy only if done for the love of God.

**The Greek philosophy :**

Clement of Alexandria says (36) : "As boys are frightened about ghosts so are many men about Greek philosophy, because they fear that it may lead them astray. . . . But David has cried out : the just man ' shall not be moved for ever.' " (37). " The Greek philosophy," says Clement, " as it were, goes before in purifying and preparing the mind for receiving the faith, and upon it truth builds up knowledge." (38). St. Augustine says : "Also even the philosophers of the Platonic school themselves, if they were to change a few of their doctrines which are condemned by Christian teaching, ought to piously bow their necks beneath the yoke of Christ the most invincible and only King." (39). " Before the coming of our Lord," says Clement, " philosophy was necessary to the Greeks unto justice ; but now it is useful unto piety. . . . For God is the author of all things good." (40). " As for the heathen sages," says Roger Bacon, " since God has enlightened their minds so as to make them perceive the truths of philosophy, it is manifest that their labour is not foreign from divine wisdom."

**Holy Childhood :**

St. Louis made his children every day hear matins, vespers, and complin, chanted in a loud tone with music, and wished them to be present at a sermon that they might hear the word of God. They were also to say the office of our Lady and to study " in order to understand the Scriptures."

**Laymen who said the Divine Office :**

Many knights and men of the world were in the habit of saying the regular office for each day. In palaces and in dungeons they loved to hear these holy words. Such was the case of St. Peter of Murrone (Pope Celestine V.), who expired in the cell of his prison in the citadel of Fumona as he finished the last psalm of lauds with the words : " Let every spirit praise the Lord." (41).

**A gift of God :**

All things beautiful in nature and art were received with thankfulness. " Beauty of body," says St. Augustine is a good gift of God : but for this reason it is bestowed on the wicked also, lest it seem to the good to be a great good." (42).

**God's little ones :**

The Church taught her ministers to treat youth with great tenderness and to forgive the sallies and levity of childhood. It would have been an evil day for children if her discipline had been abolished to make way for that of the Manicheans or Calvinists, who saw an evil principle under the most innocent appearances, and in whose breasts a dark fanaticism had killed all sweetness and mercy.

**Heights or depths :**

" The soul," says St. Gregory the great, " can never be without some delight : for it will take delight either in the highest or in the lowest things." (43).

**The open secret :**

The philosophers of the Church likewise taught men to derive heavenly wisdom and peace and hope from beholding all that was beautiful and admirable on the earth and in nature. William of Paris calls the Word Incarnate " the face of the highest beauty." Caussin says : " Would you behold God ? Observe these exquisite flowers, these waves which curl on the current of rivers, these gentle western breezes which bear comfort and health on their wings, those vast seas, that immense extent of plains, those snow-capped mountains : all things that are seen, all those that are heard, cease not to recount to us the love of our Father." So Blessed Albertus Magnus says of the vision of God : " It shall be music to the ear, sweetness to the taste, balsam to the smell, flowers to the touch. There shall be the clear light of summer, the pleasantness of the spring, the abundance of autumn, and the repose of winter." " If men should give to one person," says Eusebius Nieremberg, " all the wisdom of Solomon, all the sciences of Plato and Aristotle, all the strength of Aristomenes and Milo, all the beauty of Paris and Adonis, it would have no comparison to the delight which will be enjoyed in seeing God. In him will be found all the richness of gold, the delightfulness of the meadows, the sweet refreshment of the limpid stream, the brightness of the sun, the beauty of the heavens, the fragrance of the rose, all that can be admired and enjoyed. Everyone shall then rejoice as much in the felicity of another as in his own ineffable joy, and shall possess as many joys as he shall find companions." Even the presence of God on earth was intended to lead men to a love of things invisible, as the Church says in the preface for the Nativity : " That, whilst we know God visibly, through Him we may be rapt to the love of invisible things." In like manner all visible objects of beauty were to direct the mind to its Creator and its future destiny. " Behold the sea," says St. Ambrose (44), " look around upon the earth, that every creature made by the work of God may feed thee. What grace of forms in the very beasts ! What seemliness in men ! What beauty in the birds ! Gaze upon these things, and thou wilt behold no ' iniquity and contradiction in the city.'(45). Behold these things, and death will not enter through the windows of thine eyes." (46). And St. Augustine :

" He that made all things is better than all things. . . . Whatever thou shalt love that will He be to thee. Learn to love the Creator in the creature and in the thing made the

Maker ; lest that which is made by Him keep hold on thee and thou lose Him by Whom thou too hast been made." (47). "Who has adorned the heavens with stars," says St. Bonaventure, "the air with birds, the water with fish, the earth with plants and flowers ? . . . But what are all these things but small sparks of Thy beauty ?" (48). So when Luis of Granada is describing the change which takes place in the views which men entertain of the natural world when they have been converted to a life of piety he says : "They see all things now with other eyes, and they feel such motions and changes within as are strong proofs of every article of faith. If the nights are clear, with their eyes raised up towards the heavens they admire their beauty and the brightness of the moon and stars, considering them in a way quite different from the way in which they used to consider them, and much more joyfully. They look on them as so many mirrors of God's glory, as so many messengers that come to bring them news of Him, and they think upon those noble troops of Saints who are more bright and glorious than the stars of heaven." "Our soul," continues Caussin, "has a generous, passionate longing for Him, unless it be infected by the breath of the serpent and obstructed by vapours of sensuality. It seeks for Him, it speaks to Him in all creatures, it beholds Him in all the beautiful objects of nature. But it often falls out that it forgets the Workman in admiring the workmanship, it takes the shadow for the substance. It feels there is some invisible hand which shoots arrows at it amidst the vermilion of roses and the whiteness of lilies. Oh, how attractive is beauty ! Oh, should God's Beauty on a sudden be seen without a veil the whole world in an instant would dissolve under its adorable rays. The longing for that Divine Beauty is so naturally imprinted on the heart of man that hell itself cannot make him forget it." "This is the full blessedness and the whole glorification of man, to see the face of his God, to see Him Who made heaven and earth, to see God Who has made him, Who has saved him and Who has glorified him." (49). In this consists essentially the everlasting glory of the blessed.

**Soldiers of Christ :**

"When we are Christians," says Fenelon, "we can no

longer be cowards." The essence of Christianity is the making little of this life in comparison with that which is to come. Holy men have remarked that we find the names of more soldiers recorded in the martyrologies than of the members of almost any other profession. There is in fact a natural connection between heroism and piety.

**Polite robbery :**

" Formerly," says Sismondi, "greedy and unjust men seized the goods of others by violence ; to-day they obtain them by fraudulent bankruptcies. Every such attempt formerly was open ; to-day everything is secret." " It may be noted," says Isaac Walton, " that in this age there are people so unlike the God of mercy, so void of the bowels of pity, that they love only themselves and their children, love them so as not to be concerned whether the rest of mankind waste their days in sorrow or shame. People these that are cursed with riches and the mistake that nothing but riches can make them and theirs happy." We hear of the dungeons and chains in the castles of Chivalry, but what tales of misery and of cruelty are unfolded before the legal tribunals of the moderns !

**Voices from the tomb :**

Look at those poor dead figures on the tombs of knights, with the Cross on their breast and their armed hands raised up in prayer. Where shall we find so much religion and honour and dignity among the living as beams from that cold stone ?

# The Book of Morus

# The Book of Morus

N OLD WRITER SAYS: "THAT THE voice of the common people is the voice of God is the common voice of the people; yet it is as full of falsehood as of commonness. For who sees not these blacke-mouthed hownds, upon the meere scent of opinion, as freely spend their mouthes in hunting counter, or, like Actæon's doggs, in chasing of an innocent man to death, as if they followed the chase of truth itself in a fresh scent? Who observes not that the voice of the people, yea of that people that voiced themselves the people of God, did prosecute the God of all people with one common voice: " He is guilty of death." (50).

**A lesson on love :**

A life devoted to the study of profound philosophy had led the Count of Stolberg to the same conclusion : "Without love of God there can be no true love ; " "Ohne Leibe zu Gott ist keine wahre Liebe."

**Four snares :**

" There are four great obstacles," says Roger Bacon, " to the comprehending of truth which impede every wise man and scarcely permit anyone to arrive at the true title of wisdom, namely the example of weak and unworthy authority, daily custom, the scorn of the unlearned vulgar, and the concealment of our own ignorance with the ostentation of apparent wisdom. In these every man is involved, every state occupied."

# Maxims of Christian Chivalry

**Wise men are few :**

"The multitude of the human race," says Roger Bacon, "hath always gone astray from the truth of God, and we know that even Christian people are imperfect, for the small number of the Saints proves this. In like manner the vulgar have always been wanting in the wisdom of philosophy, for this is evident from the small number of philosophers."

**Talk instead of thought :**

Berkeley has expressed an opinion which must greatly astonish the moderns but which I believe every man of thought and learning will fully assent to, namely that : "In the present age thinking is more talked of but less practised than in ancient times. Since the revival of learning (mark the epoch) men have read much and wrote much but thought little."

**Reformed learning :**

It is generally believed that these changes (of the Reformation) in England were immediately succeeded by a flourishing state of letters. The Reformation and the revival of learning in England are made to constitute the blessed whole. But the writers of the history of English literature have shown that this was by no means the case, and that for a long time after the Reformation an effect quite contrary was produced. The grammar-schools and universities were deserted, degrees were abrogated as anti-christian. Duke Humphrey's library at Oxford was completely stripped by the spiritual reformers, and a total stop seemed to be put to all improvement in knowledge. The persons ordained by the bishops were artificers and other illiterate persons ; so that about the year 1563 there were only two divines in Oxford, the President of Magdalen and the Dean of Christ Church, who were capable of preaching before the University. Hence the humorous song :

> We'll down with all the Varsities
> Where learning is professed ;
> Because they practise and maintain
> The language of the beast.
>
> etc. etc.

86

**Heart and hand :**

When Mary Queen of Scots was led to execution she carried a crucifix, and prayed, concluding with these words: "As Thy arms, O God, were stretched out upon the Cross, so receive me into the arms of Thy mercy and forgive me my sins." "Madam," said the Earl of Kent, "you would better leave such Popish trumperies and bear Him in your heart." This was the grand charge against the Church, that she kept men from attaining to a spiritual religion. She answered: "I cannot hold in my hand the representation of His sufferings, but I must at the same time bear Him in my heart."

**A lying voice :**

"For three centuries," says de Maistre, "all history seems nothing but one great conspiracy against the truth."

**Beati esurientes :**

In a work by the amiable Father Alban Butler there is the following anecdote: "During the civil war, as the famous Marquis of Worcester was marching once in Cardiganshire, near the ruins of a monastery at Strata Florida, a woman who was a hundred years old was presented to him. She had remembered the monks in Catholic times and had lived above three score years in great regret for the loss of the public service of the altar and in constant private devotion, without seeing a priest or thinking that any priest could be found in England. The Marquis asked her: 'When the religion altered, you altered with the religion?' She answered: 'No, master, I stayed to see whether or no the people of the new religion would be better than the people of the old, and could see them better in nothing, but grow worse and worse, and charity too wax colder and colder ; and so I kept me to my old religion, I thank God, and mean, by God's grace, to live and die in it.' When the Marquis told her he would take her to Ragland Castle, his seat in Monmouthshire, where she would find a priest and might hear Mass every day, she was so transported with joy that she died before the next morning. The Marquis wept when he heard of her death and said: 'If this poor soul died where she might have served God, how joyfully will she serve Him in a place where she will never die.' "

**The power of music :**

Music is said by some holy men to have drawn the gentiles frequently into the Church through mere curiosity, which ended in conversion of heart and desire of baptism. This gave occasion to Dr. Burney to say that " the generality of parochial music with the moderns is not likely to produce similar effects, it being such as would rather drive Christians with good ears out of the church than draw Pagans into it."

**Influence of church music :**

" Whatsoever is harmonically composed delights in harmony; which makes me," says Sir Thomas Brown, " much distrust the symmetry of those heads which declaim against all church music." Socrates held philosophy to be the highest music, and to our fathers it seemed that the music of the Church was full of religion. " It consoles those that are sad at heart," says a monk of St. Gall, " it makes minds more gracious, it refreshes the studious, it invites sinners to contrition, it purifies the inward man and renders him more prompt to works of piety." What Beveridge says of himself was doubtless true of those successive generations of men who took delight in the beauty of the Lord's house and in the exercises of Catholic devotion : " Their souls became more harmonious, being accustomed so much to harmony and so averse to all manner of discord that the least jarring sound either in notes or words seemed very harsh and unpleasant to them."

**The object of church music :**

It would have been well if the modern composers of church music had philosophized more on the subject of their profession and had borne in mind the connection between the ancient style and the object to which all church music is directed. It would have been well if they had attended to the words of St. Augustine where he approves of the use of church music but observes : " Yet when it happens to me that the singing is to me more moving than the thing which is the subject matter of the song I confess that I commit a fault deserving of punishment ; and then I had rather not listen to the person who is singing." (51). Still, however, in all essential parts of the service the music of the Church continued the same, as in her prefaces, prayers, chants for the Gospel, for the Credo, and for the different offices of night and day. Here the severity of the tones added solemnity to the majestic strain, which, when accompanied with the peculiar pronunciation of the Italians, must have attained its highest beauty.

### The passion for ridicule :

In some countries in this age, there is a contemptible, certainly a most base-born, passion for making everything appear ridiculous but what serves to satisfy the ordinary wants or to gratify the grossest appetites of men. Where this awful spirit is suffered to prevail it would be hopeless to think of justifying the ceremonies of the Church or of pointing out wherein their beauty consists. Assuredly we cannot advance one step in divine philosophy, we cannot attain to the most distant conception of the spirit of the ancient religion, until this fatal leaven, destructive of all wisdom, of innocence, of love, of gentleness, of sanctity, be rooted out utterly from our hearts and thought of with horror, not only as being unholy but as being the peculiar attribute of all ignoble and base persons.

### Reverence for Scriptures :

In fact, notwithstanding all that may be rashly and ungenerously advanced by the moderns, they did the Church great injustice when they accused her of witholding a due reverence from the Sacred Scriptures. Undoubtedly, as we have before seen, she did not hold the doctrines of those who limit to the volume of Scripture the blessings promised to the Church ; and the study of the Scriptures, while recommended and practised, was not held as an indispensible requisite of a religious life.

### The Bible honoured :

Our ancestors would read the Bible on their knees. They considered, as St. Ambrose beautifully says in a passage quoted by the Count of Stolberg, that God walks through the Scriptures as if in bodily presence, and that when the sinner opens the eyes of his conscience he recognizes there the presence of God (52). " But," as the Count of Stolberg observes, "corrupt human nature hides herself from Him, as Adam and Eve hid themselves in the garden." When an emperor desired to testify his regard or reverence he could find no present more expressive than a copy of the Scriptures. The sacred volume would be in letters of gold and covered with purple and ivory and precious stones.

### Duties of youth :

St. Ambrose teaches in regard to the duties of the young that their peculiar office is "to have the fear of God, to yield respect to their parents, to honour old age, to maintain purity, not to despise humility, to love gentleness and modesty, which things are the ornaments of youth. For, as gravity becomes old men and alacrity is suited to youths, so to young men modesty belongs as if by a sort of natural gift." (53). To the young, indeed, to children, and to youths, the clergy of holy Church will be always most dear.

### Ancient piety :

"Who," says Martene, "can attentively consider the diligence of our predecessors in celebrating the divine offices, their reverence, their piety in solemnizing the mysteries of Christ, their devotion in observing the festivals of the Saints, without being incited and impelled to emulate them ? Who must not by observing their continual psalmody, even amidst manual labour, their constant meditation on holy lessons, their deep silence, their assiduous observation of prayer, be withdrawn from vain and earthly desires ? Who can read of their attention to the sick, of their solicitude for the dying, of their prayers and suffrages for the dead, without wishing to be dissolved that he may more speedily be with Christ ?"

### " Lives of great men all remind us "

"Read," says Bishop Milner, "the works of the most celebrated ascetical writers, those of a Bernard, a Bonaventure, an Antonine, a Vincent Ferrer, a Taulerus, a Gerson, a Thomas à Kempis. Peruse the accounts which have been left us of their lives, with those of their contemporaries who have been equally celebrated for their sanctity, and tell me whether the practice of all the Christian virtues inculcated by our

Saviour Christ in His divine sermon on the mountain could be more strongly recommended both by precept and example than they were by the writers and personages whom I have mentioned."

**Be not solicitous :**

You charge the ecclesiastical scholars of the Middle Age with having prevented men from attaining to that industry which distinguishes the moderns. True, the influence of the Church would operate so as to place limits to the cultivation of the commercial spirit, so as to prevent all that is sacred and holy from being sacrificed at the shrine of national wealth. It is the remark of St. Gregory the great that those Apostles who left their boats and nets to follow Christ were sometimes afterwards found in the same employment of fishing from which they were called. But St. Matthew never returned to the custom-house, because the publican's profession was a dangerous one and an occasion of avarice and oppression and extortion (54). In conformity with these views Castiglione maintains that a good prince should desire " the greater part of his people to be neither very rich nor very poor ; for the very rich," he says, " are subject to pride and insolence, the very poor to baseness and deceit." This may sound strange doctrine on the Exchange, but I marvel if it should be displeasing to kings or legislators who are not themselves mere merchants. However, the Church has had an abundant share of censure for the obstacles which she is said to have thrown in the way of heaping up riches ; and harsh things have been advanced by political economists, at least by the writers of Adam Smith's school, who seem always, as an acute observer remarks, " to regard the people as so many cattle working for an indescribable something which they call the public." Mr. Forsyth, the oracle of modern travellers in Italy, adopted these views, and he declared on one occasion the joy he experienced upon returning from dark woods and stately castle courts and vast gloomy convents to " a neat thriving town where he found a manufactory and a dinner." No doubt the music of cotton-wheels has more charms for some ears than that which is to be heard in convents. Music by itself, this writer says, " is but a sensual art, to be classed with cookery and perfumery, capable of exciting sensations but not ideas." Once for all I must declare my conviction that all parties are consistent, the moderns as well as the followers of antiquity. By the way, it is wonderful that Dr. Middleton did not avail himself of this feature in the character of the Church and confirm his comparison by quoting the classic authors. Plutarch would have furnished him with excellent parallels. Thus, speaking of the Spartans he says : " Their discourse seldom turned on money or business or trade, but upon the praises of the excellent or the contempt of the worthless." And in his comparison of Numa with Lycurgus he censures " such as place the happiness of a state in riches, luxury, and an extent of dominion, rather than in security, equity, temperance, and content." But with our men of sense, placing the happiness of a state in " security, equity, temperance, and content," is being several centuries behind in light and civilization, a pratical evidence, as they say, of the baneful, depressing, spirit of popery, which, we may admit, has been shown by the Church in every age, at least in accordance with this rule : " Let your manners be without covetousness, contented with such things as you have." (55). However, as I before acknowledged, the followers of the ancient religion of Europe, " that monstrous structure of deceit and wickedness," as an English writer of our time calls it, hold many opinions in common with the poor blind pagans. Sir John Chandos would have been more in his element on the banks of the Scamander or the Eurotas than in many places of Christendom that I could point to now.

### Whom shall I fear ?

But further, you condemn the clergy on the ground of arrogance ? Is that the term which their firmness merits ? Was it arrogance in Peter Bishop of Poitiers to excommunicate Duke William for having carried off with brutal violence the beautiful Viscountess de Chatelhérault, whom he kept concealed in his palace at Poitiers ? The Duke in a fury of rage entered the cathedral, seized the prelate at the foot of the altar, and commanded him to take off the censure under pain of death. Peter refused ; and the Duke sheathed his shining blade, saying : " I do not love you enough to send you to Paradise."

**All things in Christ :**

To the faith of a Christian and to the ancient spirit which, let controversy say what it will, is pre-eminently the meek and humble, that is, the Christian spirit, belongs everything that can command the affections, refine the taste, ennoble the imagination, and purify and sanctify the heart.

**The plague of souls :**

A violent revolution exhausts its power in one passing torrent, which sweeps away the harvest while it leaves the soil to receive future seed ; but the malignant influence of stupid sophistry is like an eastern plague, which remains a permanent source of desolation. It does not merely taint the surface of society, it takes deep root and spreads under ground and becomes indigenous. From its deadly shade the gentle and holy visions of Chivalry have fled to return no more.

**National selfishness :**

" The breaking of a glass puts us into a supreme fit of anger, and we are dull and indifferent as a Stoic when we see God dishonoured." The day of achieving a treaty that will enable us to trade with the infidels is marked with red in our calendars, and when our brethren in Jesus Christ are making a last struggle with assassins and stretching out their hands to us for help we stop our ears and sit down as cool spectators. And if a knight like Tirante should make a vow to be the first man to set his foot on land in their cause and to be the last to leave it we count him an enemy and rebellious. Their priests may be slain, their crosses may be trampled under foot at the altars. But the age of Chivalry is gone ! The nations of Christendom have broken their bond of union, have protested against their former points of fellowship, have blotted out their ancient relations ; and the sign by which the Saviour of the world declared all men might know whose disciples they are has no longer a place even in their memory.

**Roma æterna :**

" O Holy Church of Rome !" cried that virtuous nobleman the Count de Maistre in the conclusion of his admirable defence of the Roman See, " O Holy Church of Rome ! So long as I shall retain speech I will employ it to celebrate thee. I salute thee immortal mother of knowledge and of holiness."

**The day of the Lord :**
" This life," says a great modern ," is man's day in which man does what he pleases and God holds his peace. Man destroys his brother and destroys himself, and confounds governments, and raises armies, and tempts to sin, and delights in it, and drinks drunk, and forgets his sorrow, and heaps up great estates, and raises a family and a name in the annals, and makes others fear him, and introduces new religions and confounds the old ;" and changes what he owns as the fancy of the moment may require, and talks of wicked priestcraft, and affects an air of philosophy, and loves to be incredulous, and puts off self-examination as to doubts to a more convenient season, and scorns the Church, and sets up his own reason as infallible, and holds that his sincerity will excuse his errors. "And all this while God is silent." But then God will have his day too ; the day of the Lord will come, in which He will speak and no man shall answer. He will speak in the voice of thunder and fearful noises, and man shall do no more as he pleases, but must suffer as he has deserved.

# The Book of Orlandus

# The Book of Orlandus

HEN THE EMPEROR CHARLES V. desired the Marquis de Villena to lend his house to the rebel Constable de Bourbon the answer of the Castilian was, that he could not refuse gratifying his sovereign in regard to that request, but that his majesty must not be surprised if, the moment the Constable departed, he should burn to the ground a house which, having been polluted by the presence of a traitor, became an unfit habitation for a man of honour. When Jean-sans-Peur Duke of Burgundy, after the murder of the Duke of Orleans, had the audacity to return to Paris, where the King and princes were prevailed upon to see him, Louis de Clermont Duc de Bourbon was indignant at the idea of finding himself at the same court with an assassin. He rode out of Paris at the head of one hundred gentlemen of his household and, forcing his way through the Burgundian troops who were about to arrest him, took the road to his domains, where he determined to spend the remainder of his days among his dear vassals. While Henry V. of England was at Southhampton waiting to embark his troops for France, walking one day outside the walls he saw a banneret arrive at the head of one hundred and twenty knights, who saluted him saying : " Seigneur King, I come to offer you this company which I have raised at my own expense." The King, overjoyed, desired to know his name. " I am Sir William Olendyne." " A knight, without doubt ? " " No, my lord, I had embraced the monastic state, but I have forsaken the altar for a cuirass." " Deserted the altar ! " replied the King, with anger ; " you are a mis-

creant ; begone, I do not want either you or your gifts."
Olendyne embarked for France and fought against the English
at Agincourt.

### Building on sand :
" It would be easier," says Plutarch, " to found a city without
any ground for it to stand on than to form or preserve a
state without religion."

### A valiant templar :
In the time of Peter King of Arragon, when the Spanish
Admiral Roger de Luria, a Templar, arrived at the port of
Malta, where was the fleet of Marseilles, the Provençals being
taken by surprise, some of his men cried out : " Now fall
on." " God forbid," said he, " that I should attack them
while they sleep ; let the trumpet sound and I shall wait
till they are ready. Men shall not be able to say that I
attacked sleeping men." They all cried out : " The Admiral
has well spoken."

### Honour first :
The son of Philippe de Valois furnished another example
at the siege of Angoulême. Norwich defended the place,
which was not furnished with necessary supplies and which was
inhabited by friends of France. He demanded and obtained
a suspension of arms for the festival of the Purification.
" Early in the morning the gates were opened and he marched
out with all his warriors loaded with their effects, and passed
through the French army. The Duke of Normandy, bound
by his word, forbade an attack, and they withdrew in safety."

### Honour to whom honour is due :
Aristotle defines honour equally well : "Honour is the sign
of being regarded with favour ; and those are justly and
chiefly honoured who confer the greatest benefit on others."

### Motto of Chivalry :
The motto of the brave Louis, husband of St. Elizabeth of
Hungary, was that of all chivalry : " Godly , Chastely, Justly,"
" Pie, Caste, Juste."

Nobility of virtues :

Guillaume de Lalain, beginning to instruct his son, says : " With all your force and power take care to keep the commandments of God." Then he warns him against pride, anger, envy, avarice, idleness, gluttony, and luxury.

Speaking of envy he says : " No lady of honour can ever love an envious man, if he be not envious in the exercise of good virtues, in order to be the best in them, as, for example, if he wish to be in the church more devout than others, or in the company of ladies more graceful and pleasing, and more valiant in arms, whether these be of war or of the tournament.

" And know, my son, that in proportion as you come before others in nobility of lineage in the same proportion ought you to surpass them in nobility of virtues ; for the nobleness of good conduct is worth very much more than the nobleness of one's parents."

He then warns him against idleness, for of the true knight he says : " Whether it be for singing or for dancing, above all the others he is the most diligent and the most joyous ; also in getting up in the morning, in saying his hours, in hearing Mass devoutly, in going to hunt, etc. You will be reputed as a worthless fellow if you do not keep yourself within the limits of temperance in the use of wine. Then by doing thus, my son, you will live longer in the course of nature, and you will be in the grace of God so far as concerns avoiding this sin, and in His grace in regard to love also and to your Lady ; and you will have kept yourself free from this very vile and shameful sin of gluttony, and will have for your companion the sweet virtue of abstinence."

Religion and honour :

In short, religion and honour were so inseparably united that it was impossible to offend against the laws of the one without departing from what was required by the other. How fine is a description of a Duke of Normandy in an old romance : " Passynge ryche of goodes, and also vertuous of lyvynge, and loved and dred God above all thynge, and dyde grete almesse dedes, and exceeded all other in ryghtwysnesse and justyce, and moost chivalrouse in dedes of armes."

## Maxims of Christian Chivalry

**The sign of faith :**

When the Duke of Ferrara disclosed to Bayard his treacherous plan the brave knight could express his thoughts only by making the Sign of the Cross several times.

**His word was his bond :**

The honour of Turenne was so well known that most of the German princes treated with him without any guarantee. His word was enough with the English, the Swiss, the Swedes, and even the Dutch. The infidels themselves confided in the honour of our Christian Chivalry.

**The reward of worth :**

The ideas of virtue, honour, and Christian faith were so inseparably associated in the minds of the people with the character of such men that whenever these qualities were named they seemed to behold them. So when it was said in an assembly of the Greeks that a good man did not desire to seem, but to be, virtuous, instantly the whole multitude looked at Aristides.

**Dignity of Chivalry :**

The dignity which Chivalry required was removed at an infinite distance from any disdain of men and from any selfish vanity. It had no relation to the kind of honour which Aristotle says is the end of a political life, that honour by which men are made to fancy that they are good. It arose from a reliance upon God ; it was connected with all that is pure and holy, it was united to faith and love, it abode with him only as Wordsworth says :

> Who in the silent hour of inward thought
> Could still suspect and still revere himself
> In lowliness of heart.

**A soldier of the Cross :**

It still remains for us to mark that refinement and delicacy of feeling which formed so striking a characteristic of Chivalry. Of this it is easy to find examples. Don Garcia Perez de Vargas was one of the most distinguished warriors who fought at the siege of Seville, under the banner of St. Ferdinand.

One day at the beginning of the siege Don Garcia Perez and another with him were riding by the side of the river at some distance from the outposts when of a sudden there came upon them a party of seven Moors on horseback. The companion of Perez was for retreating immediately, but Don Garcia answered that never, even though he should lose his life for it, would he consent to the baseness of flight. With that his companion rode off. This moment is well described in the old ballad :

> Ha ! gone ? quoth Garci Perez ;—he smiled, and said no more
> But slowly, with his esquire, rode as he rode before.

Perez armed himself, closed his visor, and put his lance in the rest. But the enemies when they discovered that it was he, declined the combat." The honour of the action," says Mariana, " was much increased by this circumstance, that, although frequently pressed to disclose the name of the knight who had deserted him in that moment of danger, Garcia Perez would never consent to do so, for his modesty was equal to his courage." On returning to the camp he was met by Ferdinand whose first question was : " What is the name of the knight who fled and deserted you ?" " My liege," answered Garcia Perez, " ask anything else and it shall be done as I commanded. This man is already sufficently punished."

### The bloom of courtesy :

This disposition in regard to courtesy, which appeared rare and heroic to the ancients, became essential to our Christian Chivalry. Enumerating its ornaments Spenser says :

> Amongst them all grows not a fairer flower
> Than is the bloom of comely courtesy ;
> Which though it on a lowly stalk do bowre,
> Yet branches forth in brave nobility,
> And spreads itself through all civility.

### Courteous to all :

" There was no country," says Ste. Palaye, " where Chivalry did not exert its influence to promote public and private good." Nothing was little or contemptible in the eyes of a knight when it related to doing good. And he proceeds to point out that this exercise of benevolence was extended to all classes of men, even to persons of the very lowest and most abject condition. He quotes a precept of the Chevalier de la Tour, in his book of instructions, which requires the practice of courtesy towards inferiors. " Those same," he says, " will bring you greater praise and greater renown and greater good than you will receive from those in high station ; for honour and courtesy which are shown to great people are offered to them only according to their right and what we ought to do for them ; but that which is given in this way to gentlemen and gentlewomen of low estate and to those of lower standing comes from a sincere and kindly heart, and the lowly one whom we treat in this way esteems himself honoured thereby."

**Pride ruins all :**
King Perceforest in the romance, according to these principles, says to his knights : " I recall to memory a word which a hermit said to me once for my correction ; for he said to me that if I had as much in the way of possessions as the king Alexander, and as much of wisdom as the wise Solomon, and of chivalry (valour, bravery) as the valiant Hector of Troy had, pride alone if it reigned in me would destroy all."

**Strength and sweetness :**
The old historians speak of Godefroy de Bouillon as uniting " the wisdom of Nestor, the prudence of Ulysses, the valour of Achilles, the strength of a giant, with the sweetness and humility of a monk."

**Virtues make nobility :**
To noblemen it was said : " Prefer not thyself before others by reason of thy nobility, and think not those inferior to thyself who are more obscure and born in a more humble place. Our religion has no respect to persons or conditions of men, but it looks to the mind of each one. It pronounces a man slave or noble according to his ways. The only liberty in in the sight of God is not to be the servant of sins. The highest nobility with God is to be distinguished for virtues."(56)

For, as St. Francis de Sales says : " True humility never makes a show of being there, and scarcely speaks the words of humility, for it not only wishes to conceal the other virtues but also and principally it desires to hide itself. And, if it were lawful to tell a lie, to dissemble, or to scandalize one's neighbour, it would perform actions of arrogance and pride in order to hide itself under them and live altogether unknown." (57).

## Maiden modesty :

King Perceforest in the romance continues to instruct his knights and says :   " There comes to my mind a word which a holy man once said to me .  For he said in correcting me that knights and clerics ought to resemble a maiden.  For a maiden ought to be simple and modest and to speak but little ; courteous, she should be, chaste, and well-ordered in words, and in deeds kindly, polite and compassionate towards all good folk.  Knightly gentlemen, so it is in regard to you ; for if a gentleman who has received the Order of Chivalry does not resemble a maiden in graces and in virtues he ought not to be called a knight, let him be as brave as he will.  Knightly gentlemen, for this end have I spoken these words to you, that, if you wish to receive honour, you take care to resemble a maiden ; for this belongs to a knight."

## Last and first :

The rule was : " Be always the last to talk in the assemblies of people older than yourself and the first to strike in battles." " A knight, doubt it not, ought to strike high and talk low :"

> Un chevalier n'en doutez pas
> Doit ferir haut et parler bas.

## Silent humility :

Men could not praise others too much or speak too little of themselves.  " Especially it belonged to a young gentleman to speak little."  The troubadour Pierre Vidal wrote a treatise on the art of " restraining one's tongue."  The Order of " La Cosse de Geneste," instituted by St. Louis, had for motto : "He exalteth the humble (Exaltat humiles)." (58).

## *Maxims of Christian Chivalry*

**The Church prescribes courtesy :**

In taking this view of the courtesy of ancient manners it is essential to keep in mind what was shown in the second book, that it followed naturally and of necessity from the religion which prevailed in these ages. The Church prescribed it, her ministers observed it as a part of religion, children were trained to love it, both the practice and the spirit of a religious life produced it.

**Religion mother of courtesy :**

Catholic writers expressly treated of the subject of "Christian politeness." And who has ever conversed with a Benedictine or partaken of a priest's hospitality without experiencing it ? "We should respect in men the quality of the adorers of God," says an elegant writer who describes the manners of good company. Except among those of the household of the faith where is such a sentiment to be found ? The rules laid down by ascetical writers to guide novices and monks in a cloister might seem to have been composed for the instruction of nobles and princes. The rules of a monastery required humility and modesty, inattention to what is served at table, the habit of despising nothing that is offered, of complaining of nothing, of accomodating one's self to everything, of avoiding both deficiencies and excess in meals, and of correcting every indication of undisciplined appetite. These holy men were equally refined even in their gestures and carriage ; and it cannot be doubted but that whatever refinement of manners belonged to all those ages was derived in a great measure from an early education in the houses of the clergy. St. Bernard (59) and St. Ignatius Loyola prescribed sobriety, serenity, and cheerfulness of countenance. St. Jerome condemned all expressions of anger and pride (60).

**Training in courtesy :**

Courtesy was inseparable from the religious education which was received in those ages. What beautiful fruits must that spirit of yielding and of obedience have produced !

**Mother and sons :**

In the old romance of *Helyas knight of the Swan*, Ydain

Duchess of Bouillon instructs her three sons, Godfrey, Baudwin and Eustace, saying to them : "Always above all things give praise and glory to God in all your works, my fair children. Abide always in His fear and love.  Be sweet, soft, and courteous to your subjects, without opressing or damaging them in any wise.  If you be able and if it be possible you ought to rebuild the churches of God, and offer willingly your own bodies in sacrifice in sustaining the holy faith Catholic. Keep and defend justly your country.  Uphold and sustain the rights of poor widows and orphans.  Distribute and deal out of your goods to the needy, comfort the sorrowful, and think for to save your souls and for to have the grace of God. And I promise you my children that if you so govern you that you shall prosper in this world and have heaven at your end." " In such good and healthful doctrine did their good mother Ydain devoutly teach these three young sons."

### Reverence for the poor :

How many noble dames felt like Penelope that, besides the religious motive, even their dignity required them to assist and comfort all in distress who should approach them. They were not content with " writing their names in a dumb, blind book, in order placidly to rely upon an invisible board of management," but conversed with poor persons and comforted them with looks and words as well as with their purse. King Charles V. of France in giving alms to the poor would always kiss the hands of those whom he relieved.

### Horror of wrong-doing :

And remark too respecting instances of injustice and cruelty with what horror they are recorded by the old historians ; which proves how much such things differed from the actions which were in those times generally considered honourable among men.

### Kindness towards the poor :

The knights are said by the modern sophists to have been men who were never weary of oppressing and hacking the poor.  How different are the portraits which remain of these brave men !  Witness Bayard, who went about Grenoble in the time of the plague, like a priest, visiting the poor sick people and giving them medicines and food, supporting them at his own expense in hospitals, and visiting the neighbouring villages to relieve the distressed ! When was there ever a more humane and Christian sentence than his answer to those who told him that it was throwing away his money to give it to poor people in countries ravaged by war. "Gentlemen, I do that which I ought to do, let whatever can happen come to pass ! How do you know that this poor man will not be able to save his little treasure, hiding it under a tree and finding it again when the war is over, when he will pray for me ?"

**Due place for merit :**
The distinctions of rank were not suffered, as is now too often supposed, to prevent persons of merit from rising to their due places. The example of the Abbot Suger, the minister of Louis-le-Gros and of his son Louis-le-Jeune, affords occasion to Sismondi for remarking " the enthusiasm which science excited in that age and the facility with which it raised persons of the lowest class to the highest offices." Alfred exhorted the nobles to choose among their vassals such youths as should appear, by their parts and inclination to piety, particularly promising that they might be trained up to the liberal arts. As for the rest, it was not then the custom to give the poor sort much of a school education, which might abate their industry and the pleasure which they ought to take in manual labour. But this great King was careful to provide for the religious education of all.

**Poor and good :**
Meanwhile, let it be remembered that the word vilain was no disgraceful epithet, seeing it was derived by old writers from vaillant, to signify men who were companions of their lord. So that, as we read in an old romance : "Artus was committed from his birth to the care of poor and good vilains;" in which sentence, it will be well to remark the ancient phraseology of " poor and good."

**Poor and rich :**
In these ages men believed in such a thing as holy poverty,

and made vows to embrace it, and revered those who made such vows. St. Francis of Assisi, before he had embraced a Religious life, once placed himself among the poor before the gate of St. Peter's church at Rome, through love of poverty. And if the moderns would condescend to open the lives of the Saints they would see how many princes and feudal barons and knights would eat with the poor and serve them and kneel among them in prayer and after their death carry their bodies to be put into the grave. Hence the poor loved and revered the great, for the privileges of rank seemed to be exercised only for the common good.

### Poverty not a crime :

What a spectacle to behold the poor in our churches ! The poor who have escaped confinement in our humane institutions! to witness the meek resignation, the charitable unsuspicious eye, the profound devotion, of these suffering poor, lying very often prostrate on the ground at the Elevation and without strength to rise again till some friendly hand is stretched out to help them. Oh ! is it for the rich of the nineteenth century to talk of the inhumanity of the Middle Ages ? To give alms, with them, is to encourage idleness. He is hungry, he is naked ? let him work. But he is old ? there are employments for all. But he is a child ? do not teach him to beg. It is a mother of a large family ? perhaps she does not tell the truth. We have institutions on a new system. Yes truly, and woe to the unhappy ones who are doomed to receive relief from them ! In order that the children of pleasure may not be incommoded by the sight of poverty the poor are shut up within high walls and condemned to confinement for the crime of being poor and miserable. When they are thus secluded from the enjoyment of nature an odious board of governors takes care that they should be provided with what is sufficient to support life. And then they have to endure the countenances of ferocious barbarians who are the officers to administer this horrible humanity ! Our Lord named the beggar Lazarus, and the rich man he called only Dives. But now it is a shame to err or to be ignorant in naming the rich, though for the poor man it is enough if we say : " the pauper," " the vagrant," names for which we are indebted to the new philosophy.

**Family servants :**

The treatment of domestics in these ages presents another striking example of the exercise of humanity. Here again men were consistent Christians. " In the time of our ancestors," says Mr. Heber, " the interval between the domestics and the other members of a family was by no means so great or fenced with so harsh and impenetrable a barrier as in the present days of luxury and excessive refinement."

**Treatment of domestics :**

Henry II. Duc de Montmorenci had such a prodigious number of domestics and retainers that the Duchess represented to him the necessity of parting with some. The Duke pretended to agree and they made a review of his household. Whenever the Duchess named any one officer or servant as useless the Duke undertook his defence : "this man was of use to other people, that one had been recommended to him by a friend." At length there were only two whom he abandoned to his wife. " But," he added, "do you think that two persons would be a burthen to my house ? Are they not sufficiently unhappy, being good for nothing, without my afflicting them by dismissal ?" The nobility of Spain, Rome, Naples, Genoa, and Milan, used never to dismiss a domestic, but when he was disabled by age or sickness he still enjoyed his salary. The Countess d'Aulnoy speaks of nobles in Spain who had above one hundred such useless domestics. What humanity and tenderness accompanied the grandeur of the Catholic nobility ! And mark well how the character of these domestics corresponded with the affection with which they were treated by their masters.

**The king's servant :**

Guillaume de Chartres relates that during the pestilence which visited the army of St. Louis, he being in the tent with an old valet de chambre of the King, named Gangelm, who was dying, this faithful servant said to him : " I am waiting for my holy master ; no, I will not die until I have had the happiness of seeing him." The King arrived at the moment and remained with Gangelm for a considerable time, testifying the tenderest affection.

**Charity towards enemies :**

To commemorate victory by an obelisk, a bridge, or a triumphal arch, was the custom of the heathen nations, only in the most inhuman and atrocious age of their history. Our ancestors erected a cross or a chapel out of regard for their enemies.

**Hellish inventions :**

" The invention of firearms," says Sismondi, " has had consequences for the human race far more disastrous than plague or famine. It has subjected the power of man to calculation, it has reduced the soldier to the rank of a machine, it has deprived valour of its most noble part, of everything which made it personal. It has increased the power of despots and diminished that of nations, it has destroyed the security of towns, and ramparts can no longer inspire confidence." The chivalrous spirit has always manifested a horror of and contempt for such inventions.

**Then, and now !**

In 1139 Pope Innocent II., and afterwards the Emperor Conrad, forbade the use of the crossbow, which was then generally used in Italy. The French held it as too murderous an instrument for generous warfare.

**Death before dishonour :**

One is not so much struck with the display of courage in the Middle Ages as with the heroic virtue which made men devote themselves to whatever cause seemed noble and just, and made them feel that death was far preferable to the sense of having consented to dishonour.

**Generous sacrifice :**

In order that all the passions of nature might be consecrated to religion, men were anxious to devote their courageous spirit to some sacred cause, to the defence of Christian people, or to the removal of obstacles opposed to the happiness of the human race. Their zeal may have been in some instances extravagant, but it cannot be denied that, even when it needed correction, it showed a spirit the most contrary to everything selfish and ungenerous. Men were indeed more ready to admire than to criticize, when they heard how, in Shakespeare's words :

> Many a time hath banished Norfolk fought
> For Jesu Christ, in glorious Christian field
> Streaming the ensign of the Christian Cross
> Against black pagans, Turks, and Saracens ;
> And, toil'd with works of war, retired himself
> To Italy ; and there at Venice gave
> His body to that pleasant country's earth,
> And his pure soul unto his Captain Christ,
> Under whose colours he had fought so long.

**One to three :**

The rule of the Templars forbade any Knight Templar to fly before three enemies.

**Knights as religious :**

In 1211 Herman von Salza was grand-master of the Hospitallers. His heroic deeds against the infidels and his honour were celebrated through the world. Humble in prosperity, never cast down at a reverse of fortune, Hermann, as a statesman, a ruler, and a soldier, is equally great, and corresponds with the ideal of a perfect man. Such was his personal character that Pope Honorius III. and the Emperor Frederick II. chose him to be an arbitrator between them, and both showed him equal respect and friendship. It was Salza who sent Brother Hermann Balch with one hundred knights against the whole people of the Prussian infidels, three millions of bold warriors. He is described as an Achilles in bravery and an Ulysses in prudence. He conquered everywhere and founded towns. Like a lion in war, he was a mild and gracious ruler over his new people. He gave them instructors, took care of the sick, defended the priests, and gained the hearts of all.

Between 1230 and 1238 the Teutonic order under him flourished in its greatest splendour. After all its wars, Prussia, it is said, became within forty or fifty years the most flourishing and the best governed land in Europe. It has been said also that, in consequence of the institutions of the knights, the people of Prussia, in the thirteenth and fourteenth cen-

turies and the first half of the fifteenth century, enjoyed
more freedom than any German state now possesses. It is
certain that the knights in Prussia, like the Benedictine
monks in other parts, tilled the land, planted vines, reclaimed
waste fens, and erected magnificent structures. The towns
were enclosed with thick walls and towers, and more than
one thousand churches and convents were built in less than
seventy years ; facts which can hardly be reconciled with
the justice of the accusations brought against the knights by
many writers, supported as they are by vague popular tradition among the Lithuanian peasants. But however this
may be, enough has been seen to prove that the valour of
Chivalry was not the spirit of ferocious barbarians but that
of generous and devout men who were humane and lovers of
their country and disinterested benefactors of the human race.

## Fraternal charity :

Among the laws of knighthood was one by which it was
expressly forbidden to quarrel with one's companion even
though he should be in the wrong.

## Religion and courage :

"Without a sense of religion," says Gerdil, "there can be
no real courage, none that can be depended upon, none
universal, unconquerable, beyond the fear of death."

## Chivalry of La Vendée :

Our age has to boast of having produced the army of La
Vendée, which had Lescure and La Rochejaquelein for its
heroes. Their chivalrous loyalty in defence of their king has
been the subject of the memoirs of the Marchioness of La
Rochejaquelein which an illustrious German has pronounced
to be the epic poem of modern times. .

## States rest on reverence :

"If," says Jean de la Haye Baron des Couteaux, "princes,
and lords, great, courageous, and powerful, and the people
wearied with taxes, be not restrained by the fear of God,
a great state cannot last long. If he be not supported by the
reverence instilled by the prelates of the Church, excellent in

manners and doctrine, it is not possible that one king can restrain them ; for force will be his enemy, and the strongest will wish to be king."

### The charm of modesty :
The modesty of the chivalrous character preserved our ancestors from that spirit of ridicule and disdain which their descendants have so generally adopted in reference to their companions and brethren.

### Private and public life :
Upon the whole then we may conclude that the feelings and judgment, if not the theories and doctrines, of antiquity, led men to hold to the rule of Chivalry with respect to the conduct of friendship. The heart taught them what cannot be better expressed than in the words of Æschines, in which he alluded to his great rival, saying : " He who is a bad father can never be a good public leader ; nor can he ever love the people who does not love those who are near and precious to him. He who is a bad man in private life can never be good in public life." But good or useful work may of course sometimes be done in public by a bad man ; and not all bad men are wholly bad or without any natural good quality.

### Friendship in Middle Ages :
In the Middle Ages the system of education, whether in cloisters or castles, was fruitful in this beautiful plant of friendship. " The connection," says Büsching, " which a long intercourse necessarily produced, knit together by the double bonds of benefit and gratitude, became indissoluble. Hence Chivalry produced so many bonds for life and death and for ever. Children were to repay the benefits conferred upon their fathers, and so they stood by their benefactor or by those who succeeded him." Neither rank nor riches interfered with the cultivation of generous friendship.

### Cultivate right feeling :
Pierre Vidal the troubadour thus advises a companion : " Prefer among young men those who have feeling ; they are always desirous of honour and are naturally magnificent.

Keep company with such as are of manly age, provided that they think with nobleness, that they love grave men, such as praise virtue and combat vice and have an inclination to whatever is good. Shun those whose manners are corrupt and whose tastes are low. In them you will find a sovereign contempt for poets. Still some few men of this character repent after a long time and amend their lives ; and it is better to associate with them than with proud, stupid, rich people, who are daily more and more puffed up with wind. Shun those who join a revolting brutality to some talent, and who delight in low company. You will find other barons who think of nothing besides drinking, eating, and sleeping. Shame is all that can be gained in their company." The maxim of Godfrey of Bouillon :

> Who fears no God he loves no friend,

was repeated in every instruction to youth. The same sentiment occurs in the *Golden Fleece :* " If he is not faithful and loyal to God he cannot be so to men."

### St. Chrysostom on friendship :

Of friendship St. John Chrysostom says : " This plant has its roots in Heaven." (61). It grows with the spiritual growth of men, it is strengthened by the silence of meditation, everything that belongs to religion and genius feeds and nourishes it, for example the music of evening choirs, the peaceful aspirations of the soul, the adorable Sacrament of the altar. " Friendship which can come to an end," says St. Jerome, " never was true friendship." (62).

### Friendship comes from heaven :

" What is there that a true and brotherly friend will not do for his friend ? what pleasure will he not bring to him ? what utility ? what security ? Even though you will speak of treasures that cannot be counted there is nothing which can be compared with a true and brotherly friend. Firstly then we will say how great is the pleasure which belongs to friendship. A friend is transported with joy and gladness when he sees his friend ; he is united to him with a kind of union which is fraught with ineffable delight for his spirit ; and if he only recalls the memory of his friend he rises up and is exalted in his mind. I speak of brotherly friends who are of one soul, who would be willing to die for each other. Think not that you can tell me the meaning of what is here said if you have in view friends who love but slightly, who are but table friends, friends only in name. If any one has a friend such as I speak of he will know the meaning of my words. If he sees such a friend every day this will not be enough for him ; he wishes and prays for the same things on behalf of his friend which he wishes for and prays for on his own behalf. Hence I have known one who used to ask holy men to pray first for his friend and then for himself. . . .

For in truth a friend is more to be desired than the light of day itself. I speak of a sincere and brotherly friend. Nor oughtest thou to wonder at this ; for it were better that the sun should cease to shine on us than that we should be without friends. And in what sense do I say this ? Many who see the sun are in darkness ; but those who possess friends are never overcome by troubles. I speak of spiritual friends, who place nothing before friendship. . . .

I know that there are many who do not understand what is here said ; and the cause of this is that I am talking of a thing which now dwells in heaven. For in like manner as if I were speaking of some plant which grows in India, of which not one of my hearers knew anything by experience, no speech of mine could explain to them the nature of that plant, though I should speak without ending, so too, whatever things I shall now say I shall say in vain ; no one will know my meaning. In heaven is that plant of friendship planted, and the branches which it has are laden, not with pearls, but with the power of life, which is a fruit much more delightful than pearls." (63).

### Symposia :

The following remark of the Count de Maistre may serve as an apology for the custom of King Arthur's court, still, in some measure, preserved in England : " I regret much those symposiums of which antiquity has left us some precious memorials. Women are charming without doubt ; to avoid becoming savage one must live with them. Large assemblies have their value ; it is well to consent to them with a good grace. But, I am of opinion that, when all the duties have been discharged which are imposed by custom, men would do well to meet together, to converse even at table. I know not why we do not imitate the ancients in this respect."

**Royal frugality :**
If we view the interior, to pass over the skins and rushes of which Diodorus Siculus speaks, we find in the castle of René d' Anjou, the most magnificent prince of his age for tournaments and public entertainments, a few wooden chairs or benches and some curtains of coarse blue stuff. Montesquieu found no other kind of furniture in the household of the prime minister of the Grand Duke of Florence ; and the poet Gray says that in the Palazzo Doria in Genoa the " furniture seemed as old as the founder of the family." It is true some embossed silver tables proclaim in bas-relief his victories at sea, how he entertained the Emperor Charles V., and how he refused the sovereignty of the commonwealth when it was offered to him ; but all the rest consists of some old-fashioned chairs and Gothic tapestry. Ulysses was a skilful boat-builder and he made his own bedstead. The Emperor Maximilian used to sit in a chair which he had made himself, which may be seen to this day in Germany. The grounds too of great men in the Middle Ages were laid out for use rather than for pleasure ; for the wild woods and rocks afforded them the greatest pleasure. Charlemagne's garden could boast only of a few lilies, roses, poppies, and heliotropes. In one of his capitularies he orders all surplus of his vegetables and his fowl to be sold.

**Knighthood begins from childhood :**
Büsching quotes a saying of Tristan : " Knighthood must begin from childhood. Honour requires bodily sufferings, and comfort is the ruin of honour when we indulge in it too long or too much."

**Gifts of the cedar :**
Thus Philopoemen spent his time between agriculture and the study of philosophy ; a mode of life which, in the Middle Ages, was considered as divine and religious and conducive

to the perfection of saints. The passion for glory could induce Alexander to pour water upon the ground which his fainting soldiers had carried to him in a helmet when they were passing through the Gedrosian desert. The spirit of sacrifice in the Middle Ages produced deeds equally heroic. Agesilaus held that a prince should excel ordinary men in being able to endure the summer's sun and the winter's cold. This was the education which formed men like the old Roman, " with a mind unconquerable, of rigid innocence, and despising riches, in abstinence and patience of labour of an iron frame, and soul ; " or like the spaniard, who, as Landor says, "has the qualities of the cedar, patient of cold and heat, nourished on little, lofty and dark, unbending and incorruptible."

**Chivalrous discipline :**
   Büsching remarks that " the habit of obedience, the principle of which was derived from the patriarchal ages, thus learned in youth, was a noble preparation for subsequent command. The progress to knighthood was long and gradual ; nothing sudden hurried the boy from an unwarlike service to the life of peril. Every one had to obey and learn, so that step by step he might become familiar with the dangers and troubles of a chivalrous life."

**Bare heads and feet :**
   Thus Henry IV. of France used to go bareheaded on the mountains and without shoes or stockings like the other children of the province. Du Guesclin went barefoot in his youth. Bavo-le-Brun, Governor of Hainault, is said by Jaques de Guyse to have required all from the age of six to fifteen to go barefoot.

**Wrong training at home :**
   Montaigne even objects to the education of children by their parents, because, he says, these latter are unwilling to see their son " fed on coarse food as he ought to be and without delicacy." And he adds in conclusion : " For there is no remedy for it, he who wishes to make of his son a worthy man must needs without doubt risk a little in this age of youth and often offend against the rules of medicine."

**Hardy through hardship:**

The old Lord Gray, to fit his sons for the hardships of war, would usually in the depth of winter, in frost, snow, rain, and what weather soever fell, cause them at midnight to be roused out of their beds that they might go a-hunting till the next morning. Then perhaps they would come home wet and cold, to have for breakfast a brown loaf and a mouldy cheese. The monks of St. Denis say that Charlemagne, during a long winter's night, used to go to bed and get up again four or five times.

**A lesson from Nuns:**

The man in the old play who reckons the want of a pillow among the evils of poverty would have amused knights like old Sir Ewan Cameron of Lochiel who kicked a snowball from under the head of his grandson. Garci Fernandez Manrique, who was famous for often surprising the Moors during the night, had founded the convent of St. Salvador de Palacios de Benagel for Benedictine nuns. He used to shame his men if they ever complained of his hours by reminding them of the holy sisters and their matin bell.

These were the habits which enabled our ancestors to rival the ancients in the vastness of their enterprises.

**The best inheritance:**

A gentleman once asked Bayard what inheritance a father was bound to leave his children. " He should leave to them," he answered, " the mind that fears neither rain nor tempest nor force of man nor human injustice ; and that is wisdom and virtue."

**Die standing:**

" We are born for action," says Montaigne, " and not only an emperor but every gallant man ought to die standing."

**Trotting boys:**

When the Cid travelled from Valencia to the Cortes at Toledo there went with him five hundred esquires on foot, all hidalgos, besides those who were bred in his household.

## Maxims of Christian Chivalry

**Serving on foot :**

Albert relates that many of the most noble knights in the Crusade of which he writes, having lost their horses, continued to serve on foot. Here again was an exercise replete with pleasure for those who were in that short but precious moment of life when, young as they were, vigorous, full of health, of security, of confidence in themselves and in others, an expansive fulness extended as it were their being through all their sensations and embellished to their eyes the whole of nature with the charm of their existence. They too would have confessed that when they travelled on foot, "in guise of trotting boys," (garçons trotereaulx), like Lancelot and Mordrec in the strange forest, it was in their happiest days.

**Arthur's ride :**

In the Romance of Arthur of Little Britain there is a fine example of the spirit which prompted these expeditions. "So it fortuned on a night that Arthur, in his father's castle, Hector, and Governar, were all three lodged in one chambre. And Arthur was sore troubled in his sleep, and turned and sighed many times, so that Hector and Governar heard him and sayd each to other: 'Arthur is not well at his ease, let us go wake him.' And then Governar woke him, and asked him what he ailed ? 'O frende Governar,' said Arthur, ' I have be sore troubled in my sleep, for I dreamt that I was far out of this country.' 'O Sir,' said Hector, ' we ought to go into strange countrys ; for before this time ye have promised so to do. Therefore set your mind no longer to tarry at home, but shortly let us depart.' 'As God help me, cosin,' said Arthur, ' the day is come that for to have the city of Paris I will tarry no longer ; for to-morrow will I ask licence of my father and of my mother, and I will have with me no more company but you and Governar and Jacket my squire. 'Sir,' said Governar, ' ye say well ; for a young man without pain is little worth.' So they departed and rode long and had many adventures."

**Nature points to heaven :**

Moreover under the influence of the Catholic religion the wish of the religious Wordsworth had been realized to the traveller of the Middle Ages. Cliffs, fountains, rivers, seasons, times, had all reminded his soul of heaven.

**Honour to women ;**

In Tancredus I spoke of the religious graces which distinguished the women of those ages. In this place it remains for us to view them still more as they show themselves under the peculiar influence of Chivalry. The greatest enemies of the feudal system have acknowledged that the preponderance of domestic manners was its essential characteristic. In the early education of youth, women were represented as the objects of respectful love and the dispensers of happiness. The child was taught that to be an honourable and happy man he should prove himself worthy of the love of a virtuous woman. "This lesson," says Ulrick von Lichtenstein in his book entitled *Duties owed to Women*, "every boy sucked in with his mother's milk ; so that it was not wonderful that love and honour should become identified in his soul. When I was a child so young that I used to ride upon a stick I was fully persuaded that I ought to honour women with all that I possessed, love, goods, courage, and life." Till the age of seven the child was to be under the discipline of women. Wirnt von Gravenberg in his chivalrous poem of Wigolais relates, that, while the knights would teach the boy all the exercises of Chivalry, the women of the castle had such an affection for his virtue that they allowed him when much older to go about in a familiar manner among them. Büsching laments that with the decline of Chivalry this tender and at the same time this manly education should have been changed for a mode which did not profess to secure the attainment of any such general object. Religion and the rules of Chivalry conspired in those ages to convince youth that the object of its pride was to be obtained by virtue, that the image which was beheld with all the rapture of the imagination was to be approached in the discharge of duty, and that, while infidelity might present its temptations to the senses, whatever the heart held dear in time and in eternity was connected with its faith in Christ.

Ulrich von Lichtenstein speaks of himself as follows : "They gave me a master who was rich in high virtue, the

Margrave Henry of Austria, who served women with full loyalty and spake ever nobly of them as a knight should. He was mild, bold, and of high heart, wise with the wise, and foolish with the foolish. He endured labour for the sake of honour, and his mouth never spake a bad word. To all his friends he was generous and faithful, and he loved God from his heart. This worthy master said to me, whoever would live well must give himself up to serve a woman. He taught me much of his gentle virtue, how to speak of women, how to ride on horseback, and how to compose sweet verses. He said, thereby will a young man endear himself to people when he can praise women with gentleness, and when he loves them dearer than himself ; for, said he, that which arises from a flattering and lying mind can never succeed with the good. Had I fulfilled all that he said to me I should have been worthier than I am." It is expressly recorded of Louis de Clermont Duc de Bourbon that he would never remain in any place where words were uttered aganist a woman ; and in his noble speech to the knights who were assembled at Moulins to be invested with his new Order of Hope he said : "All who belong to this Order must honour women and never speak or hear evil of them, for those who so speak are cowards. Under God, part of the honour of the world proceeds from women." Thus in a famous romance, when the Marshal of Myrpoys ridiculed Arthur for being led by the hands of ladies after the tourney this knight answered : " Syr, yf these ladyes take me by the hand I thank them therof ; for it is by their courtesye and not by my deservynge. Therefore I love them the better, and wyll be the gladder for to serve them, and to be a faythful knyght to them al in general. For, as God help me, so moche is a knyght worth as he can deserve prayse of ladyes and damoyselles." They can even impart noble and generous sentiments, so that their power exceeds that of Kings, who can grant only the titles of nobility. The eyes of women were like a star to youth. When in the romance Perdiras and Lionnel sent the two pages, whom they had saved in the forest, to Queen Idore wife of Perceforest, the knights say of her : " Know that she is such a very good lady and in such sort has in herself all manner of honour and courtesy that there are no young knights or esquires

120

who ought not to wish to be of her household by reason of the goodness and honour which those may learn who are near her. For there is no gentleman so dull and rude that he cannot find in her the way of honour and courtesy."

The general maxim was : " Lost is all honour to him who does not render honour to woman." And Büsching remarks that everything in the education of boys tended to raise to the highest degree that reverence for women which had distinguished old Germany. That education softened and refined the manners of youth and made the mind generous and the person graceful, by requiring a constant and, at the same time, a willing and cheerful obedience. Tacitus says that the Germans thought there was something holy in women, and that they never despised their counsels or neglected their answers. How remarkably was this spirit shown by St. Louis when the sultan enquired what money he would give for his ransom, and he answered " It is for the sultan to explain himself. If his proposals are reasonable I will make the Queen acquainted with the terms enjoined." The infidels were lost in astonishment at such respect for a woman. "It is," replied the king, " because she is my lady and my companion."

### Fidelity and love :

Marsollier has written the life of the Duchesse de Montmorenci whose tragical history conveys such an example of fidelity and love. In his last hours the Duke Henry II. at Toulouse manifested the most profound piety. He made a general confession and received Holy Communion. " My Father," said he to the Jesuit Father who assisted him, "when one has received the Author of life within one's roof, one has no more fear of death." He wrote to his wife in these terms : " My dear heart, I bid you the last adieu with the same affection which we have always cherished for each other. I beseech you, by the repose of my soul, which I trust will soon be in heaven, that you will moderate your resentment and receive this affliction from the hand of our sweet Saviour. I receive so many favours from His goodness that you have great grounds for consolation. Once more, my dear heart, adieu !" Pope Urban VIII, the senate of Venice, the Duke of Savoy, Charles I. of England and Henrietta his Queen, all interceded for him, but his execution was hurried on before many of the letters could arrive. He heard his sentence with heroic tranquility. "Gentlemen," he answered, " I thank you and your assembly. Be assured that I regard this sentence of the King's justice as a decree of God's mercy." He was glad to offer his life in expiation. He chose to be bound and to be meanly clad that he might imitate Jesus Christ in the circumstances of His Passion. The Duchess, the unfortunate Marie-Felice des Ursins, loved her husband with a passion which could scarcely be surpassed. No one dared to relate to her the event of the Duke's execution till two Capuchins brought her the letter which he had written to her in his last moments. Upon recovering her senses from a long swoon, after the first agony of her grief had subsided, she remembered his last charge to forgive their enemies and she sought her only consolation at the foot of the crucifix. "O my God," she cried, " I loved only him in the world, and you have taken him away, that I might love only you." Eight days after the execution she received orders to leave Languedoc for one of three places, of which she chose Moulins. Passing by Lyons she was reduced to the necessity of selling the horses belonging to her carriage in order to be able to continue her journey. On arriving at Moulins she was shut up in the castle. But soon she was permitted to fix her abode in a large house in a retired place outside the town. There she remained in a room hung with black and lighted only by a few tapers. Her only employment was in consoling the miserable. " I believe," she said, " that no one is more unhappy than myself, but this does not render me insensible to the sad condition of the unfortunate. Her family, one of the most illustrious in Italy, in vain endeavoured to prevail on her to return to Rome. After ten years King Louis XIII. passing by Moulins sent a gentleman to compliment her. The messenger was struck with awe on entering this place of mourning. " Testify to the King," she said, " that I am surprised he should remember an unfortunate woman unworthy of the honour he shows her ; but fail not to describe to him what you behold." With these words she burst into tears. The Cardinal de Richelieu sent his page to visit the Duchess. She answered with the same grief and moderation : " Tell his Eminence

that you have found the widow of the Marshal de Mont-
morency weeping still, after ten years, on the tomb of her
spouse." After the death of the king she built a noble church
for the nuns of the Visitation at Moulins, in which she raised
a superb mausoleum to the Duke ; and his remains were
removed to it from Toulouse. She then took the veil and
became the abbess and a great benefactress of the poor.
She was destined to console a number of illustrious persons
in misfortune. It was in her bosom that the Queen of
England Henriette of France poured forth her sorrows for
her husband. With her the Duchesses of Longueville and
Châtillon sought the calm and peace which they could not find
amid the agitations and intrigues of the court. She died in 1666.

**A wise woman :**

In every house at a certain stated hour all the women assembled in the chapel with the mistress of the family, there to
recite the rosary aloud. " The infante Namfos," says
Raymon Muntaner, " had for his wife one of the most charming
persons of Spain, the daughter of the noble En Gonbau
d' Entença. She was one of the wisest women in the world,
and one might make a great book composed of the instances
of her wisdom. She was a right excellent Christian and one
who did much good in her life for the glory of God. She passed
away in the city of Saragossa, and was buried on the day after
that of her death, that is to say, on the festival of the Blessed
Apostles Sts. Simon and Jude, in the church of the Friars
Minor. God in His goodness receive her soul as that of a
blessed and holy woman ! She had received all the sacraments
as a good Catholic and as one pleasing to God and to all the
world."

**Qualities which retain affection :**

Duke Philip, in an old romance, begs a knight to tell him
what made him love his wife best. " Well syr," said he,
" I shall show it unto you. I love her because she is gracious
and gentyle of heart, for her grace and gentyl heart hath me
retayned unto her service, in so moch that I quyte all the
world for her, For, as help me God, I have found in her,
grace, gentylness, and sweetness."

**Not masculine :**
" In women," says Castiglione, " their manners, words, gestures, and air, ought to be peculiar to their sex ; for, as only solid and manly qualities become the man, so a more soft and delicate form recommends the woman. A certain female sweetness ought to shine in all her manner, that, whether she walk or stand or speak, she may appear without any mixture of the masculine."

**Mildness and grace :**
The perfection of the female character was regarded as consisting in angelic mildness and delicate grace, incapable of a thought which bordered on cruelty.

**A brave queen :**
The lords of the village of Chatenai refusing to set free several unhappy villagers who were languishing in prison, the pious mother of St. Louis at the head of her people went to burst open the gates. Before the Revolution the stick was still preserved with which she struck the door and commenced the attack with her own hand.

**Hector's courtesy :**
Hector feared the reproaches of the Trojan women more than the spears of the Greeks, and the affecting testimony which Helen bears to his gentleness when lamenting his death is proof that in his delicate regard for women he resembled a most perfect knight. One would think that he must have heard the lessons of our Chivalry as delivered in the fable of Constant du Hamel, where it is said : " I cannot pardon you for having ridiculed women. All one's life one is bound to honour and serve them, and never to speak to them but with the utmost courtesy. Who acts otherwise is a low fellow."

**True dignity :**
" There is a kind of superiority," says Ségur, " which women should preserve over us, arising even from their weakness and the respect which it inspires. There is another kind which belongs to the dignity of man, which not only do women recognize, but for the abandonment of which they

never pardon him." It was from this latter truth being lost sight of that arose the absurd and pernicious cases of base influence which, at a later period, were the scandal of certain courts. But Chivalry was directly opposed to this abuse of female influence.

## Woman's right place :

It was with husbands who resembled young lovers, rather than indolent, selfish persons, like the prince in Tirante the White who was afraid to follow the King's daughter lest he should sully his robe, that women partook in their hearts of all joys and sorrows. And though the change from one climate to another had stained their limbs and the sun had drawn a cypress over their foreheads, yet their wives deemed them comely and fair. Women, sustained by the hand of Chivalry in the place appointed by their Creator, prompted men to the pursuit of virtue.

> For love does always bring forth bounteous deeds,
> And in each gentle heart desire of honour breeds.

## Encouragement from sympathy :

When the Scots besieged Werk Castle, belonging to the Earl of Salisbury, " ther was a sore assaut and a perylous," says Froissart. " Ther might a ben sene many noble dedes on both partes. Ther was within present the noble Countesse of Salysbury, who was as then reputed for the most sagest and fayrest lady of all England. This noble lady comforted them greatly within, for by the regarde of such a lady, and by her swete comforting, a man ought to be worthe two men at nede."

## Woman's discourse on Chivalry :

When the Emperor in the romance of Tirante the White saw his daughter conversing with Diofebo, " matters are going on well," he said, " for when women discourse upon Chivalry knights become more worthy." This was the charm which enabled Jason of old to conquer. Without this the castles of Chivalry were but ill fortified. As King Alexander says to Sibille : "A house is very desolate which is without a woman."

## A father's legacy :

The father of the Maréchal de Boucicaut, "who was a very righteous man and of great knowledge, did not trouble himself about amassing wealth or about anything else except acquiring honour." It was this valiant gentleman who answered his relations when they were blaming him for not endeavouring through his interest at court to obtain lands and dignities for his children : " I have sold nothing, nor have I thought of selling the inheritance which my father left me. I have acquired nothing, nor do I wish to do so. If my children be righteous and valiant they will have enough, and if they be worthless it will be a pity that they have what remains to them."

## I came to serve :

Dom Joam de Castro had not money to rebuild the fortress of Dio, which was to save India and to be the foundation of his glorious renown. In this emergency he wrote from Dio to the Council of Goa stating his distress and concluding thus : " I earnestly beg of you to lend me 20,000 pardaos, which, as a gentleman I promise, and on the Holy Gospel swear, before a year's end, to see repaid to you. I commanded the taking up of my son, Dom Fernando, whom the Moors killed in this fortress (fighting for God and our Lord the King), to pawn to you his bones, but they were found so that it was not fitting to take them out of the ground. So I am without any other pawn but part of my beard, which I here send you by Deigo Rodrigues de Azevedo. As you know I have neither gold, plate, nor anything of value to secure your property, only a plain and naked truth given me by God Almighty. I commend myself, Gentlemen, to your goodness. Dated at Dio, the 23rd of November 1546." The merchants furnished him with more than he demanded. After his glorious triumph as Viceroy of India he wrote to the King desiring leave to return to Portugal and begging for two acres of ground which rose into a hill above his country house at Cintra, which to this day is called the Mountain of Good News. The Infante Dom Luis in his letter to Dom Joam implies that he wanted these tops of the rocks of Cintra only that he might build chapels upon them. It was the King's wish, however, that he should stay for three years longer in India. But his long exertions and hardship caused him to sink suddenly under the pressure of so arduous a command. When seized with his mortal sickness he summoned the bishop and the chancellor of the state and the chief magistrate of the city, the Guardian of the Franciscans, and St. Francis Xavier, before whom he made this speech : " I am not ashamed, gentlemen, to tell you that the Viceroy of India wants in his sickness those conveniences which the meanest soldier finds in the hospitals. I came to serve not to traffic in the East. I would to yourselves have pawned the bones of my son, and did pawn the hairs of my beard, to assure you that I had no gold or plate. There was not this day money enough in the house to buy me a dinner ; for in the fleets which I sent forth the soldiers fed upon the governor's salary before the King's pay, and it is no wonder for the father of so many children to be poor. I request of you during the time of this sickness to order me a becoming maintenance." Then asking for a missal he took his oath on the Gospel that he was not debtor one crusado to the King, or to any Christian, Jew, Moor, or pagan. As soon as he found that he was in danger he secluded himself with St. Francis Xavier who prepared him for his end. Having received the Sacraments of the Church he gave up his soul to God on the 6th of June 1548 in the forty-eighth year of his age. In his study were found three pieces of small money, a discipline, and the locks of his beard which he had pawned. This was the sum of his riches after he had governed India with such glory and benefit to his King. So devoutly did he reverence the Cross of Christ that he rather chose to build a temple to its memory than raise a house to his posterity. So he left it, on his father's blessing, to his son Dom Alvaro, that, if he found in the King's favour any recompense for his father's services, he should with that build a convent for the Franciscans on the mountain of Cintra and name the house after the Holy Cross. His son faithfully carried out his injunction.

**Religious Orders of Knights :**

The Religious Orders of knighthood furnish an illustration

which more immediately belongs to Chivalry. Men of noble birth, who might have received the homage of the world and availed themselves of all its pleasures, upon entering the Teutonic Order or that of the Temple, were from that moment to consort with the companions of poverty. Within the majestic walls of Marienburg, water and bread and an old cloak were all that the new knight received in exchange for his worldly possessions. A small cell or a chamber which he had to share with a brother of the Order, which no fire ever warmed in winter, was his habitation ; a sack and a pillow of straw formed his bed. The holy offices of the Church were to be attended both night and day. Tournaments and all the expensive diversions of the world were strictly denied to him. His amusement was that which belonged to poverty, to assemble with his companions in a great hall and practise games which required strength and agility. Here indeed he enjoyed the happy world of friendship and nature. The statute-book of his Order reminded him that he would have this reward, where it said : " Love is the foundation of spiritual life, it is its fruit and its recompense. Without love neither Orders nor deeds are holy. Love is a treasure ; the poor man who can obtain it is rich and the rich man who is without it is poor." But what a life of apparent sacrifice and privation was that of the knights ! Yet these were the men who accomplished those prodigies, who drained those immense plains, who raised that prodigious bank against great waters, who constructed that stupendous aqueduct, who built those magnificent churches, which assuredly gave rise to a debt of gratitude which can never be discharged. Well may later ages regard their way of life as hardly support-able, inconceivable, and even full of terror. Nevertheless, for this life did the sons of princes and the first nobles of Europe renounce the pleasures and the splendour of the world, receiving in exchange for riches and secular pomp, by means of a spotless life of purity and obedience, a treasure even of present happiness and a title to everlasting renown.

**Nobility not in possessions :**
Of Bayard the old writer of his life says : " He esteemed in his heart a perfect gentleman who had an income of only

a hundred francs as much as a prince who had a hundred
thousand ; and he kept this before his mind that possessions
do not make people noble.  If a knight was but ill-mounted
he could console himself with remembering that the valiant
Riccar Loghercio rode a mule to battle, and that at the battle
of Antioch many of the noblest crusaders rode upon asses.

**Littleness of a few acres :**
When, as Plato says, the whole earth is full of charms why
should we confine our attachment to a few acres ?

**Happiness not in riches :**
" Wordly riches," says St. Augustine, "do not make either
ourselves or our children happy, those riches which are either
to be lost while we live, or when we die, possessed by those
whom we know not, or by those perhaps whom we should
not wish to possess them ; but God makes us happy, Who is
the true wealth of our minds." (64).

**The world's greatest treasure :**
The feelings of Chivalry, like those of youth, rendered
men careless of the pleasures resulting from riches.   Friendship was the dearest of its worldly treasures, and poverty was
a bond and a test of friendship.   "Cease now," says Boethius,
" to seek the wealth that has been lost ;  you have found
friends and in them the most precious kind of riches."   Tirante
the White in poverty learns who it is that loves him.

**Poverty and taste :**
In matters of taste too. poverty was no obstacle to our
ancestors.   The dark figure of the Templar without any
gold on his spurs or bridle had as imposing an air as the
splendid panoply of a Duke of Burgundy mounted on his white
charger with trappings of embroidered velvet bordered with
golden bells.   "No poet makes mention of golden spurs,"
says Petrarch ;  " with iron indeed I am familiar."   Amanieu
des Escas gives minute instructions to a young squire respecting his dress.   " If you are not rich enough to have a handsome
robe let there be nothing slovenly in your girdle, stockings,
and shoes ;  and then you need not be troubled, provided

I

your locks be neatly dressed. Your robes had better be torn than unsewn ; for the first only indicates a slender fortune whereas the latter denotes a bad education. Nothing pleases more or has more the air of courtesy than to be dressed well at a small expense, when one has not a great fortune, and you will arrive at that perfection by keeping good company."

**Humility in greatness :**
While Godfrey of Bouillon lay before Arsuf certain eastern chiefs from Samaria came to present him with gifts. They found him sitting upon some straw expecting the return of some knights whom he had sent out to seek provisions. The chiefs did not conceal their astonishment at beholding a prince before whom the whole East trembled not surrounded with any pomp or clad in costly apparel. But Godfrey answered that a mortal man may well be content to have the earth for his seat while alive which after his death will be the habitation of his body. The easterns praised this humility and affirmed that Duke Godfrey was worthy to rule all nations of the world.

**Money not an end :**
" I am not the King of gold," said the Emperor Maximilian to his father, " but of men." The epithet of " Maximilian the moneyless " might indeed have indicated a culpable neglect of economy, which would be dangerous in a sovereign. For though it is but little to learn that it was used of him as a reproach by the vulgar class of mankind, we are yet obliged to respect the judgment of the impartial historian. But it must be repeated, as it has been again and again proclaimed by every man who has wished to promote the virtue of his fellow-men, that the temper of mind which despises money, which regards it as an instrument and not as an object, which is neither overjoyed at its presence nor afflicted at its loss, is a virtue of the very first importance in the human heart. This temper of mind will for ever be the pride and the badge of nobility, and it will ensure to those who possess it a more sovereign and a more proud dominion than even the crown of an empire or the sceptre of the Caesars can give.

**Better give than have :**

It is thus that Hixem the Arabic king of Cordova expressed his mind : " The hand of the noble is open and liberal ; the love of gain is incompatible with greatness of soul. I love the flowery garden and its sweet solitude. I love the zephyr of the fields and the smiling beauties of the meadow. But I do not desire to be the owner of these things, for heaven has given me treasures only that I may dispense them."

**Nature a temple :**

Our Catholic ancestors placed their abbeys in similar situations, which afforded to men that most perfect pleasure of enjoying at the same time the loveliness and peace of a country life and the delights of solemn worship amidst affecting solemnity and holy song. Their surrounding woods too, contained oracular trees, like those of Dodona, which could pronounce lessons of wisdom. Oh what a moment was that when on the dewy lawn, in some natural amphitheatre of wooded hills, as day arose, in that sweet hour, one heard the chant of lauds from some abbey, mingled with the liquid tones of the nightingale ! What more could have been found in those happy islands which were thought to lie in the ocean, so delightful that they seemed intended for Gods and not for men, so greatly did they abound in beauty and joyful inspiration ! St. Bernard at Clairvaux used often to go out after the office of the night was sung and walk through the wood which surrounded the monastery till it was time to sing the morning office ; and this interval he would spend in prayer for his brethren. Once, at this hour, he had a vision of angels descending into the valley from the mountains.

These holy men, living in the bosom of nature, were examples to the world of the excellence of uniting a love of nature with the Christian faith.

**Flowers speak of Heaven :**

Anne de Montmorenci Constable of France, on retiring from court, passed his time at Chantilly occupied with agriculture and the care of flowers. The distinctions of nature were observed by such men before those of society ; youth was to respect age, and rank wisdom. Men learned to hope for another life in which they could possess all joys and perfect beauty. Deeply as they were imbued with a love of nature they were not so deceived as to expect from it what it could never yield; and they wanted not examples to prove the vanity of rustic retirement and of the pleasures of literature when left without those resources which only can secure the light and peace of the soul.

### Light from the " dark ages "

The Middle Ages have been styled the dark ages in reproach, to signify the ignorance in which, it is said, men were then universally involved. I propose to examine the justice of this charge and the principles which are used in supporting it. And now, in the first place, it must be confessed that a taste for reading was not a characteristic of the warlike youth who in those ages were employed in defending Christendom or in protecting the weak and oppressed. The renowned Du Guesclin, who saved his country, had never learned to read, and the heroic Bayard was certainly not a man of letters.

### What is ignorance ?

Socrates asks: "What is really ignorance?" He does not answer: "When any one is not familiar with what certain sophists have said or written," for there ends knowledge in the ordinary acceptation of the term; but his answer is: "When any one does not love but on the contrary hates what is good and honourable while he loves and embraces that which is evil and unjust." "Good men," he continues, " are to be deemed wise and able men and fit for government although they may not know their letters."

### What readest thou ?

But it may be asked, how can there be manly dignity, how can there be honour, how can there be the high disdain of baseness, without which there can be no virtue, when the mind receives its only food from the pages which are prepared for the multitude, containing the words of base, clever men, who make literature an affair of money, having prosperity for their God ?

**The book of the Cross :**

What a rage now for books ! Christ left no written instructions behind Him, being pleased to give us Himself on the Cross instead of a book. " Take care to remark," says St. Jerome, " that not only all those things which are recorded in the Scriptures, which the Holy Ghost enumerates as having happened on earth, but also those things in the heavenly regions which are hidden from us, are all contained and summed up in the Passion of Christ." (65). Jesus on the Cross was a devout book which the wisest men studied without ceasing, to learn the practice of the most heroic virtues.

**Worth of learning :**

Truly, upon religious grounds, experience proves that learning does not merit for its own sake such great reverence as it sometimes receives. Gold and power can often outweigh truth in the estimation of the learned themselves. They praise what is honourable but they adhere to what brings profit. The wife of Hero asked Simonides whether it was better to be rich or wise. " To be rich, surely," said he ; " do you not see the wise dancing attendance in the porticos of the rich ?"

**Aided by the simple :**

Bossuet says that all the good which is done in the Church, and even that which is the work of her pastors, is done with the help of the secret sighs of those innocent dove-like souls who are scattered over the face of the earth (66).

**Praises of the unlettered :**

Henry I. de Montmorenci, the true lover of his country, could neither read nor write. His generous and heroic soul was the admiration of the world. Such was his ability and knowledge of the human heart that Henry IV. of France used to say : "With the help of my godfather, who does not know how to read, there is nothing that I cannot undertake." The knights and barons were unlettered and ignorant ; be it so. But were they on that account less capable of understanding the duties which they had been born to fulfil ? Had they less faith ? Were they less generous, less meek and humble, less devoted to religion and virtue ? Cicero knew that there had been many men without learning of excellent virtue. He even adds : " Nature without learning oftener attains to virtue and praise than learning without nature." Raphael is not said to have been a man of letters ; yet how divine and noble the spirit which animated his forms ! What a sense must he have possessed of nobility, beauty, modesty, and grace ! Would mere reading and knowledge have sufficed for his soul, when, a short time before his death, he painted his last work, the Saviour enveloped in a glory emanating from the fountain of eternal light, and surrounded by that chaste and celestial radiance which in its fulness is reserved for the eyes of the elect ? Raphael was the painter of mind, and if, in his art he reached such heights of the sublime, it is proved that without learning and knowledge of literature men can rise to intellectual sovereignty.

### Wisdom from lives of Saints :

Pausanias, with all his learning, was credulously super-stitious, and he even denied the immortality of the soul. Surely facts like these might reasonably lead men to the opinion which Muratori did not disdain to profess, that " the lives of the Saints are, of all human books, the most useful to read." It was these which used to be read aloud in the chapters of the religious orders of knighthood.

### Modern " enlightenment ! "

Compare the simple character of our unlettered, and, if you will, ignorant ancestors, with the mind of those who now pride themselves on their superior knowledge. Look at the pomp of learning, the insolence of flattered talents, which lead the men of today to look with such contempt upon the peasants of a Catholic land. See the veil of refinement which is thrown over dishonourable thoughts and base passions, the distaste which removes men from the softening influence of domestic life. A remorseless selfishness now prevails, unsubdued by the habit of yielding to the wish of others, with a calculating and compromising so-called prudence which looks to nothing but pleasure and profit while it boasts of a foundation in the principles of an enlightened philosophy.

A spirit of mean concession and compromise is abroad, which is ever ready to worship the rich and powerful, and to consign the wrongs of the innocent to oblivion. We have now that principle, the curse of a reading age, which leads men to idolize the acuteness of intellect and to despise the virtues of the heart. In a word we have in this age the disposition and the principles which have been substituted for those of Chivalry and for all those generous thoughts and holy feelings which bound men to their religion and to their country. When such a contrast between the spirit of the ages of Chivalry and that of our own time presents itself it is hard not to think and speak in a way which is inconsistent with the respect which is due to the intellectual faculties of the soul.

**Pliny's age and ours :**
Pliny, describing his own unhappy age, asks, who now is ready to yield to authority ? " Immediately they are wise," he says, " immediately they know all things : they have reverence for no one, they follow the example of no one, and each one of them is an example for himself."

**Religion never dies :**
The scholar may indeed instruct a few by his researches, the philosopher may astonish the world by the justice of his calculations, the man of letters may give a kind of polish and a momentary charm to society, but he who is possessed of simple faith and of high honour, whether he be a Red-Cross knight or only some shepherd lad, is, beyond all comparison, the more proper object of affection and reverence. His qualities, his acquirements, are more or less connected with the immortal part of his nature. " Everything else," says the incomparable Fenelon, "dies." Then, alluding to religion, he adds : " It never dies."

**Truth always precious :**
There is no kind of knowledge whereby any part of truth is seen but our ancestors accounted it precious, whether it be that Egyptian and Chaldean mathematical wisdom wherewith Pope Sylvester and Roger Bacon were furnished, or that natural, moral, and civil wisdom which appears in the writings

of St. Gregory the Great and St. Thomas, or that oratorical wisdom which St. Chrysostom and St. Bernard displayed after the example of St. Paul, or that Judaical wisdom which St. Jerome learned with as much zeal as if, like the same holy Apostle, he had sat at the feet of Gamaliel. To detract from the dignity of wisdom would have seemed to our ancestors to injure even God Himself, to Whose praise all things were to be reduced.

### Accomplished women :

Büsching remarks that in the time of greatest ignorance women were more accomplished than men, having more opportunity of acquiring knowledge. In fact devotion stimulated them to acquire a knowledge of the Latin tongue. Many examples confirm this opinion of their learning. St. Louis was perfectly master of the Latin tongue in consequence of the care of his mother Blanche. This princess was a daughter of Alphonso IX. King of Castile, the great conqueror, who in the battle of Muradal defeated the Emir Mahomet, called the Green, with an army of above 200,000 Moors. Godfrey of Bouillon, eldest son of Eustache II. Count of Boulogne and Lens and of Ida, daughter of Godfrey the Bearded Duke of Lower Lorraine and of Bouillon descended from Charles first Duke of Lower Lorraine who was brother of King Lothaire of the race of Charlemagne, derived his love of learning from his mother. He spoke and wrote elegantly the Latin, Teutonic, and other languages.

### Value of reading :

Rudolph of Hapsburg being presented by a citizen of Strasburg with a manuscript describing the wars of the Romans against the Germans bestowed on the author a gold medal and chain which he was accustomed to wear round his neck. His answer to the complaints of his relations who reminded him that the troops wanted their pay is strikingly character-istic of that great man : "Would to God I could employ more time in reading, and could expend some of that money on learned men which I must throw away on so many illiterate knights !"

The school of travel :

Not even the travels of Chivalry were suffered to interfere
with the interests of letters. This can be easily believed by
those who remember the incessant journeys of Plato, Cicero,
and Erasmus. These travels may have conduced to ends still
more important than the immediate interests of literature,
since, as Montaign says, " there is no better school than to
propose a diversity of modes of life, and to impart a knowledge
of the variety of the forms of nature."

A sinful silence :

Religion pronounced that there was a sinful silence. " There
is a silence sinful," says Robert of Sorbon, "where man seems
to acquiesce in all manners. And of such men the world says
that they are wise and liberal, because they know how to keep
on the best relations with men of every kind." " But these
men," he continues, " are like bats, the vilest and most
hateful of creatures, of which no man can pronounce what
they are. We read that of old the bat waited to see whether
the beasts or the birds would gain the victory that she
might then share with the conqueror. Being caught by the
beasts she showed her four feet and said : ' I am one of you ' ;
and when she was among the birds she showed her wings and
so passed for a bird among them."

No vain frivolity :

The noblest writers of the French nation are willing to
deny that the charge of levity can be proved against the
character of their countrymen of former times. " The idle
life of the court," says Barante describing that life in the time
of Louis XIV., " and the conversation of women, had destroyed
that character of gravity which formerly belonged to the
French, and had introduced a frivolity which since that
period has increased." Certainly the Joinvilles and Châtillons
may be adduced in proof of this proposition. True to nature,
the writers of the romances of Chivalry ascribe, without
perhaps being aware of it, the same character to their heroes.
The knights of the Round Table are for ever wandering
among perilous forests and dark sierras.

**Sadness an element of greatness :**

Aristotle remarked that all the great heroes and geniuses of the world had been inclined to melancholy ; and he cites the examples of Hercules, Lysander, Socrates, and Plato.

**Medieval devotion to the Passion :**

At the main root of all that was devout and heroic in those ages lay profoundly engraven the remembrance of the Passion of Christ. St. Bonaventure says that St. Francis of Assisi would remain in solitary places filling the groves with his groans and bedewing the ground with his tears, and that sometimes he was heard with a loud voice lamenting over the Passion of the Lord as if it were placed there visibly before him (67). Only the impious can be insensible at the spectacle of the Cross.

**The shadow of the Cross :**

The two most triumphant days of our Saviour's mortal life seem to be that of his Transfiguration and that whereon He made His magnificent entry into Jerusalem. And yet on the latter occasion He wept as if moistening His triumph with tears, and on the former Moses and Elias, who appeared beside Him, spoke of that which He was to fulfil in Jerusalem. These were the reflections which moved the knightly soul. That voice of their Lord sounded for ever in the ears and in the inmost hearts of the faithful : "Attend, and see if there be any sorrow like to my sorrow." (68). At the piteous image of our Lord's Cross they were ready to repeat the invitation : " Let us also go, that we may die with Him." (69.) Let us not ask again why that darkness was upon the spirit of Chivalry, why the young were taught to bind chaplets of roses round their brows in semblance of the sorrowful crown of thorns, why the gloom of ancestral towers was to strike with awe the frivolous sons of laughter-loving gaiety inhabiting the domes of novelty and song, why yews and cypress trees cast their mournful shadows over the sweet garden. Children of pleasure, it was in a garden that Christ was betrayed and taken captive by the Jews. And let us not wonder why death is still encompassed with mournful trophies and solemn tones of deep compassion, for Christ departed with a cry : "With a strong cry and tears." (70).

**Domine dirige nos !**

The soul of man while it remains estranged from its true
bent is restless like the troubled sea and dark as the night of
death. The heart is torn asunder and dissolved by earthly
desires. Witness the sadness of Tiberius, morose and sus-
picious ; witness the gloom of the modern poetry, full of
bitter regret for past joys, without any bright and enlivening
prospects for the future, emitting only one dreary sound,
" like the wind through a ruined cell," only satisfied when it
can shake confidence, only eloquent in doubt, only mighty
in destroying the beautiful images which its own genius has
produced, and which it seems to hate as soon as it has given
them birth.

**The end crowns all :**

Behold the prospects of the Christian Chivalry ! the object
and end of its eventful course ! The star of honour is lost
in the bright beams of eternal truth and justice. For honour,
" that choicest, most essential essence of our purest and
loftiest humanity," rises only out of the affections which are
called into life by danger and uncertainty. The service of
Chivalry is at an end : its career is finished. For it had been
the labour, for men the advantage, for God the glory. Therefore with our heroic fathers let us ever cry : " Perish our
honour, perish our glory, perish our ease, perish our life, let
us perish wholly, THAT GOD'S GLORY MAY LIVE."

Such words should finish every noble and joyous book that
would breathe the spirit of the CHRISTIAN CHIVALRY.

# Appendix

**1.** St. John XVIII. 37.    **2.** These words and those which are printed in capitals on page 73 represent the two fundamental and essential elements in what may be called the sublime edifice of Christian Chivalry.    **3.** Catechis. Conc. Trid. pars. II. Quæst XXIII. De Sacr. Ordinis.    **4.** Oratio II. n. 91 Migne P.G. 35, 499.    **5.** De Sacerd. III. 4. Migne P.G. 48. 642.    **6.** De Dig. Sacerd. c. 5, Migne P.L. 17, 577.    **7.** St. Paul II. Tim. III. 1-2.    **8.** In Ps. 85 n.6, Migne P.L. 37, 1085.    **9.** Epis. lib. I. ep. 5, Migne P.L. 77, 450.    **10.** This passage is attributed by Digby to St. John Chrysostom ; but for the present purpose it has not been found possible to verify it. The want of an adequate index to Migne's edition of the works of the Fathers makes the verifying of some citations a difficult task.    **11.** Introd. a la Vie Dévote III. Part. chap. IV.    **12.** St. John VIII. 36.    **13.** St. John XI. 12-14.    **14.** Habacuc III. 17-18.    **15.** Ps. LXXII. 25-26.    **16.** De Civ. Dei V. 26, Migne P.L. 41-173.    **17.** Form. Honest. Vit. n. 2, Migne P.L. 184-1167.    **18.** As these lines and some others which appear in the text are written in old French it may be well to give a translation :

> Knights in this world of ours
> Cannot live without care :
> Their duty it is to defend the people
> And to shed their blood for the faith.

**19.**

> That one ought through his chivalry
> To win a bed in Paradise
> Which God grants to his friends.

> To hold to purity in the body
> If he wish to come to God.

That you ought to shed your blood
And fight in defense of Holy Church.

Death and the earth where you will lie
Whence you came and whither you will go.

That you always have a brave spirit
To serve God for all the time of your life.

That he ought to protect the poor people,
So that the rich may not be able to cheat them,
And he ought to hold up the weak,
So that the strong may not be able to confound them,
Which is a work of mercy.

**20.** Psalms V. 8. **21.** " Into thy hands I commend my spirit:
Thou hast redeemed me, O Lord, the God of truth."—Ps. XXX.
6. **22.** Roman Ritual, prayers for the dying. **23.** Migne P.L.
In. Epist. Joan. ad Parthos. **24.** Psalms CXI. 2. **25.** Ec-
clesiastes IX. 16. **26.** St. Paul, Titus II. 12. **27.** Isaias
XXXIX. 8. **28.** Psalms XI. 2 **29.** Roman Ritual, prayers
for one who has just died. **30.** Ep. 106, Ad Magistrum
Henricum Murdach n. 2, Migne P.L. 182, 242. **31.** De
Virginibus II. 2, Migne P.L. 16, 208-09. **32.** See above
note 2. **33.** St. Elizabeth of Hungary. **34.** St. Matthew
V. 3. **35.** De Adventu Domini Serm. IV. 5, Migne P.L. 183,
49. **36.** Stromata VI. 10, Migne P.G. 9, 302. **37.** Psalms
CXI. 5. **38.** Stromata VII. 3, Migne P.G. 9, 426.
**39.** Ep. 118 Ad Dioscurum n. 21, Migne P.L. 33, 442. **40.**
Stromata lib. I. c. V. Migne P.G. tom. I. **41.** Psalms CL.
5. **42.** De Civ. Dei XV. 22, Migne P.L. 41, 467. **43.**
Moral XVIII. 9 (8), Migne P.L. 76, 46. **44.** In Psalm
CXVIII. Serm. V. n. 28, Migne P.L. 15, 1261. **45.** Psalms LIV.
10. **46.** Jeremias IX. 21. **47.** In Psalm XXXIX. n. 8,
Migne P.L. 36, 439. **48.** Soliloq. c. I. 3, 12 Ed. Quaracchi
1893, tom. VIII. p. 33. **49.** Attributed by Digby to St.
Augustine. But see above note 10. **50.** St. Matthew
XXVI. 66 and XXVII. 22. **51.** Confess. X. 33, n. 50,
Migne P.L. 32, 800. **52.** Ep. 49 n. 3-4. **53.** De Officiis
I. 17, Migne P.L. 16, 42-3. **54.** Hom. 24 in Evangelia.
**55.** St. Paul Hebrews XIII. 5. **56.** In Migne's edition of
the works of the Fathers the letter which contains this fine
passage is attributed to St. Jerome (see Migne P.L. 22, 1214).

But this letter is not in fact by St. Jerome. **57.** Introd. a la Vie Dévote III. part. chap. V. par. 4. **58.** St. Luke I. 52. **59.** Formula Honest. Vit. n. 4, Migne P.L. 184, 1169. **60.** See Ep. 38 n. 2, P.L. 22, 464. Ep. 76 n. 1, P.L. 22, 689. Ep. 108 n. 18, P.L. 22, 893. Super Joel Proph. c. I. v. 5. **61.** In Ep. I. ad Thess., Hom. II. n. 4, Migne P.G. 62, 405. **62.** Ep. III. ad Ruffinum n. 6, Migne P.L. 22, 335. **63.** In Ep. ad Thess. Hom. II. n. 3-4, Migne P.G. 62, 403-405. **64.** De Civ. Dei V. 18 n. 1, Migne P.L. 41, 162. **65.** In Ep. ad Ephes. Migne P.L. 26, 454. **66.** Serm. sur l'Unité de l'Eglise. *cf.* S. Aug. De Bapt. Contra Donat. III. 17, Migne P.L. 43, 1498. **67.** Legend S. Francisci c. X. ed. Quaracchi 1898 tom. VIII. p. 534. **68.** Lamentations I. 12. **69.** St. John XI. 16. **70.** Hebrews V. 7.

To his charitable Brethren and to other kind Friends, for much needed help, the Editor offers thanks as the expression of his heart-felt gratitude.

### SIT NOMEN DOMINI BENEDICTUM
#### Amen.

Lightning Source UK Ltd.
Milton Keynes UK
UKHW031121021122
411510UK00002B/489